THE VOLUNTARY AID SOCIETIES

St. John
Ambulance

St. Andrew's
Ambulance
Association

British
Red Cross

POCKET
FIRST
AID

Tl

D1332861

DORLING KINDERSLEY
LONDON • NEW YORK • SYDNEY • MOSCOW
www.dk.com

A DORLING KINDERSLEY BOOK

www.dk.com

St. John Ambulance, a registered charity, St. Andrew's Ambulance Association, a registered charity in Scotland, and the British Red Cross Society, a registered charity, receive a royalty for every copy of this book sold by Dorling Kindersley. Details of the royalties payable to the Societies can be obtained by writing to the Publisher, Dorling Kindersley Limited at 9 Henrietta Street, London WC2E 8PS. For the purposes of the Charities Act 1992 no further seller of the Manual shall be deemed to be a commercial participator with these three Societies.

VOLUNTARY AID SOCIETIES' CONSULTANTS

Sir Peter Beale, Chief Medical Adviser, British Red Cross
Dr Lotte Newman, Medical Adviser, St. John Ambulance
Bill Gallagher, Training Adviser, St. Andrew's Ambulance Association

Design	Kelly Flynn
Project Editor	Claire Cross
Senior Managing Editor	Corinne Roberts
Senior Managing Art Editor	Lynne Brown
Consultant Editor	Jemima Dunne
Senior Art Editor	Karen Ward
Production	Maryann Rogers

First published in Great Britain in 1999 by Dorling Kindersley Limited, 9 Henrietta Street, Covent Garden, London WC2E 8PS

Illustration copyright © 1999 by Dorling Kindersley Limited
Text copyright © 1999 by
St. John Ambulance; St. Andrew's Ambulance Association;
The British Red Cross Society

A CIP catalogue record for this book is available from the British Library

ISBN 0-7513-0709-2 (Paperback)

Reproduced in Singapore by Colourscan

Printed in Hong Kong by Wing King Tong Co. Ltd.

CONTENTS

4 Introduction

INTRODUCTION

This first edition of Pocket First Aid responds to a demand for a compact reference book that will be more readily accessible at a medical emergency. The book covers essential first-aid techniques in detail, from life-saving resuscitation procedures to the dressing of wounds. All of the material in the book has been taken from the revised 7th edition of the *First Aid Manual* written by the same authors and published by Dorling Kindersley.

Clear photographic illustrations enhance your understanding of the step-by-step advice given for each first-aid procedure. This advice has been based on guidelines agreed and issued internationally in 1998 for first-aid treatments and resuscitation techniques.

It is stressed that the practice of effective first aid is based on knowledge, training, and experience. In order to feel as confident as possible in, perhaps, the saving of a life or limb, why not complete an instruction course such as that provided by St. John Ambulance, St. Andrew's Ambulance Association, or the British Red Cross, resulting in the award of a First Aid Certificate?

HOW TO USE THIS BOOK

Introduction describes likely causes and effects of the injury or illness

Your aims in giving each first-aid treatment are summarised

DO NOT boxes warn you against actions that may endanger the casualty and harm yourself

Photographs show first-aid techniques

Colour-coded chapters help you find relevant information quickly

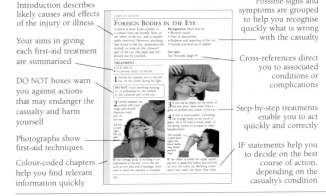

Possible signs and symptoms are grouped to help you recognise quickly what is wrong with the casualty

Cross-references direct you to associated conditions or complications

Step-by-step treatments enable you to act quickly and correctly

IF statements help you to decide on the best course of action, depending on the casualty's condition

FIRST AID AT AN EMERGENCY

Working to a clear plan during an emergency will help to ensure that you are effectively prioritising the many demands upon your attention.

Do not become distracted by non-vital activities. Bear in mind the main steps of emergency action – *Assess, Make Safe, Give Emergency Aid,* and *Get Help*.

- ✦ Control your feelings.
- ✦ Take a moment to think.
- ✦ Do not place yourself in danger.
- ✦ Use your common-sense.
- ✦ Do not attempt too much alone.
- ✦ Be aware of potential dangers such as gas or petrol: use eyes, ears, and nose to look for clues, for example the hiss of gas or smell of petrol.

ASSESS THE SITUATION

Your approach should be brisk, but calm and controlled, so that you can quickly take in as much information as possible. Your priorities are to identify any risks to yourself, to the casualty, and to any bystanders, then to assess the resources available to you and the kind of help you need. State that you have first-aid skills. If there are no doctors, nurses, or experienced people present, calmly take charge. First ask yourself these questions:

- ✦ is there any continuing danger?
- ✦ is anyone's life in immediate danger?
- ✦ are there bystanders who can help?
- ✦ do I need specialist help?

MAKE THE AREA SAFE

The conditions that caused the accident may still present a danger. You must put your own safety first. You cannot help others if you become a casualty.

Often, simple measures, like turning off an electric switch, will make the area safe. Sometimes more complicated procedures are required. Never put yourself or the casualty at risk by attempting too much.

Dealing with ongoing danger
If you cannot eliminate a hazard, try to put some distance between it and the casualty. As a last resort, remove the casualty from the danger. In many situations, you will need specialist help and equipment.

First switch off ignition, even if engine is not running

TELEPHONING FOR HELP

You can summon help by telephone from a number of sources.

◆ *Emergency services* (999): police, fire, and ambulance; mountain, cave, mine, and fell rescue; HM Coastguard. The European Union emergency number, 112, is also valid.

◆ *Utilities*: gas, electricity, and water.

◆ *Health services*: doctor, dentist, nurse, or midwife.

If you have to leave a casualty alone, take any vital action first to minimise risk to him or her. Make your call short but accurate.

FINDING A TELEPHONE

Emergency calls are free, and can be made on any telephone, including most mobile and car phones. On motorways, emergency telephones can be found every mile; marker posts between them indicate the nearest box. These telephones simply need to be picked up to be answered.

Most large companies have special arrangements for calling for assistance. Make sure that you are familiar with them. If you ask someone else to make the call, ask them to come back and confirm that help is on the way.

MAKING THE CALL

On dialling 999, you will be asked which service you need, and will be put through to the appropriate control officer. If there are casualties, ask for an ambulance; the control officer can contact other emergency services.

Give the accident details (*see right*). If unsure of your location, do not panic – your call can be traced to any phone, except mobiles. Do not put the phone down until the officer clears the line.

You may be required to stay by the telephone to "lead in" the emergency services. If you delegate this task, make sure that the person understands its importance and reports back to you.

CALLING THE EMERGENCY SERVICES

Think, and give clear, concise details

State your name and that you are acting as a First Aider.

If you have time, give the operator the following details:

◆ Your telephone number.

◆ The location of the incident; a road name or number, if possible, and junctions or other landmarks.

◆ The type of incident, for example, "Traffic accident, two cars, road blocked, three people are trapped".

◆ The number, approximate ages, and sex of the casualties, and what you know about their condition, for example, "Man, fifties, suspected heart attack, cardiac arrest".

◆ Details of hazards such as gas, hazardous substances, power-line damage, or bad weather conditions, for example, fog or ice.

RESUSCITATION

1

For life to continue, oxygen must enter the lungs and be carried to the body cells via the bloodstream. If the brain does not have a constant supply of oxygen, it will begin to fail after a few minutes. With no oxygen, a person will lose consciousness, heartbeat and breathing will cease, and death will result.

The ABC of life

Three elements enable oxygen to reach the brain. The *Airway* must be open for oxygen to enter the body; *Breathing* must occur so that oxygen enters the bloodstream via the lungs; and the *Circulation* must carry blood to tissues and organs, including the brain.

Resuscitation techniques

The priority is to establish and maintain breathing and circulation. This chapter tells you how to assist a casualty whose breathing or heart has stopped. The technique used to sustain life in this emergency situation is called *Cardio-pulmonary Resuscitation* (*CPR*).

FIRST-AID PRIORITIES

- Keep the brain supplied with oxygen by following the ABC of resuscitation: open the Airway, and maintain Breathing and Circulation.
- Obtain professional medical help urgently.

PRINCIPLES OF RESUSCITATION

To sustain life, a constant supply of oxygen must be delivered to the brain and other vital organs by the circulating blood. The "pump" that maintains the circulation is the heart. If the heart stops (cardiac arrest), urgent action must be taken if death is to be prevented.

In some cases, a machine called a "defibrillator" (see page 38), carried in most ambulances, can start the heart beating again, so you should inform the medical services if you suspect cardiac arrest.

Survival is most likely if:
◆ the flow of oxygenated blood is rapidly restored to the brain by means of artificial ventilation and chest compression (cardio-pulmonary resuscitation or CPR);
◆ a defibrillator is used promptly;
◆ the casualty quickly receives specialised treatment in hospital.

CPR is unlikely to restart a stopped heart, but it must be carried out. If applied correctly, it will keep the circulation going and ensure a blood supply to the brain until help arrives.

Cardiac arrest – the chain of survival
The casualty's chances of survival are greatest when all the following steps are taken.

Early access	Early CPR	Early defibrillation	Early advanced care
Help is summoned so a defibrillator arrives as soon as possible.	Resuscitation is given before expert help arrives.	A controlled electric shock is given to jolt the heart into a normal rhythm.	Specialised treatment quickly stabilises the casualty's condition.

THE ABC OF RESUSCITATION

A is for **AIRWAY**
To "open the airway", lift the chin and tilt the head back. This lifts the tongue off the back of the throat so that it does not block the air passage (see page 11).

B is for **BREATHING**
If a casualty is not breathing, oxygenate the blood with "artificial ventilation": blow your own exhaled air into the casualty's lungs (see page 14).

C is for **CIRCULATION**
If the heart stops, apply "chest compressions" to get blood into the heart and around the body. Combine with artificial ventilation to oxygenate the blood (see page 16).

THE RESUSCITATION SEQUENCE

When dealing with a collapsed casualty, following the sequence below will enable you to check the casualty's response, breathing, and circulation, and show you how to resuscitate if necessary.

CHECK CASUALTY'S RESPONSE

Talk to him and gently shake him to see if he responds. If there is no response, shout for help.

OPEN THE *AIRWAY*; CHECK BREATHING

Tilt the head back to open the airway (*see page 11*). Check for breathing (*see page 11*).

IF the casualty is breathing, place him in the recovery position (*see page 12*).

BREATHE FOR THE CASUALTY

Look into the mouth and remove any obvious obstruction (*see page 15*). If the casualty is not breathing, keep the head tilted back, pinch the nostrils closed, and give two breaths of mouth-to-mouth ventilation (*see page 14*).

ASSESS FOR *CIRCULATION*

Feel for a pulse for up to ten seconds. If present, continue ventilations. If there is no pulse or other sign of recovery (*see page 16*), give CPR.

COMMENCE CPR

Alternate 15 chest compressions to two breaths of artificial ventilation. Repeat this sequence as necessary (*see page 16*).

WHEN TO CALL AN AMBULANCE

IF you have a helper, get him to call an ambulance immediately.
IF alone, breathing is absent, and the casualty has been injured or drowned, resuscitate for one minute then call an ambulance. For other adult casualties with no breathing, call an ambulance then resuscitate until help arrives.

RESUSCITATION TECHNIQUES

To assess and treat a casualty who has collapsed, use the resuscitation techniques outlined on the following pages. If breathing and pulse return at any point, place the casualty in the recovery position (see page 12).

THE RESUSCITATION SEQUENCE				
CHECK RESPONSE	OPEN AIRWAY AND CHECK BREATHING	BREATHE FOR THE CASUALTY	ASSESS FOR CIRCULATION	COMMENCE CPR

CHECKING RESPONSE

On discovering a collapsed casualty, establish whether he is conscious or unconscious. Ask a question such as "What has happened?" or give a command such as "Open your eyes!". Speak loudly and clearly in his ear and gently shake his shoulders. If there is no response, shout for help then open the airway (see opposite page).

Gently shake shoulders

IF a collapsed casualty responds you must establish the level of consciousness: see AVPU code below. Monitor his condition until he recovers or help arrives as he may drift in and out of consciousness.

ALWAYS assume there are head or neck injuries; handle the head carefully and only shake the shoulders very gently.

THE AVPU CODE
A fully unconscious casualty will not respond. A partially conscious man may move slightly or mumble. Assess him with the AVPU code:

A - Alert
V - responds to Voice
P - responds to Pain
U - Unresponsive.

CHECK POINTS
Observe the following:
Eyes: do they remain closed?
Speech: does the casualty respond to the questions you ask?
Movement: does the casualty obey commands or respond to a pinch?

Record your findings on a Glasgow coma scale chart (see page 128).

OPENING THE AIRWAY

An unconscious casualty's airway may become narrowed or blocked. This makes breathing difficult and noisy, or completely impossible.

The main reason for this is the loss of muscular control in the throat, which lets the tongue fall back, blocking the airway. Lifting the chin and tilting the head stops the tongue blocking the airway so that the casualty can breathe.

Blocked airway
Unconsciousness relaxes the muscles and the tongue falls back blocking the airway.

Open airway
Chin lift and head tilt raise the tongue from the back of the throat, leaving the airway clear.

TO OPEN THE AIRWAY

Placing two fingers under the point of the casualty's chin, lift the jaw. At the same time, place your other hand on the casualty's forehead, and gently tilt the head well back.

IF you think that there are head or neck injuries, handle the head very carefully to avoid injuring the casualty further. Tilt the head back very slightly – just far enough to open the casualty's airway.

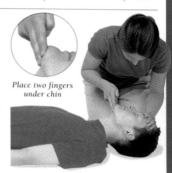

Place two fingers under chin

CHECKING BREATHING

Kneel beside the casualty, and put your face close to his mouth. Look, listen, and feel for breathing.
* Look along the chest to see if the chest rises, indicating breathing.
* Listen for sounds of breathing.
* Feel for breath on your cheek.
Do the above checks for up to ten seconds before deciding that breathing is absent.

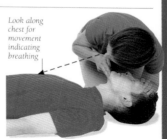

Look along chest for movement indicating breathing

THE RECOVERY POSITION

An unconscious casualty who is breathing should be placed in the recovery position. This stops the tongue blocking the throat, and allows liquids to drain from the mouth, reducing the risk of the casualty inhaling stomach contents.

The head, neck, and back align and the limbs support the body in this position. If you have to leave the casualty to get help, he or she can safely be left in this position.

The technique, below, assumes that the casualty is found on his back. Not all the steps will be necessary if he is lying on his side or front.

See also:
Spinal Recovery Position, page 78.

METHOD

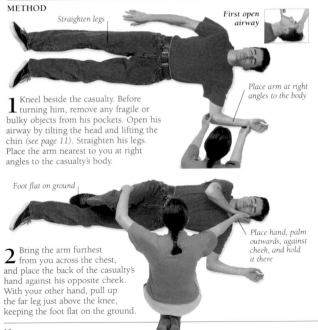

Straighten legs

First open airway

Place arm at right angles to the body

1 Kneel beside the casualty. Before turning him, remove any fragile or bulky objects from his pockets. Open his airway by tilting the head and lifting the chin (*see page 11*). Straighten his legs. Place the arm nearest to you at right angles to the casualty's body.

Foot flat on ground

Place hand, palm outwards, against cheek, and hold it there

2 Bring the arm furthest from you across the chest, and place the back of the casualty's hand against his opposite cheek. With your other hand, pull up the far leg just above the knee, keeping the foot flat on the ground.

Pull bent leg towards you

Tilt chin to drain mouth

3 Keeping the casualty's hand pressed against his cheek, pull on the upper leg to roll the casualty towards you and on to his side.

4 If necessary, use your knees to support the casualty so that he is prevented from rolling too far forwards.

Bent leg props up body and prevents casualty rolling forward

Hand supports head

Make sure head is tilted well back

5 Tilt the head back to ensure the airway remains open. If necessary, adjust the hand under the cheek and adjust the upper leg so that both the hip and the knee joints are bent at right angles.

6 ☎ DIAL 999 FOR AN AMBULANCE.
Monitor and record breathing and pulse every ten minutes until help arrives.

MODIFYING THE RECOVERY POSITION FOR INJURIES
A casualty with a spinal injury needs extra support at the head and neck, and the head and trunk need to be aligned at all times (*see page 78*). If limbs are injured and cannot be bent, place rolled blankets around the casualty, or get helpers to support him, to stop him toppling forwards.

13

| THE RESUSCITATION SEQUENCE | | | | |
| CHECK RESPONSE | OPEN AIRWAY AND CHECK BREATHING | **BREATHE FOR THE CASUALTY** | ASSESS FOR CIRCULATION | COMMENCE CPR |

BREATHING FOR THE CASUALTY

Oxygen keeps body cells alive. Exhaled air contains about 16% oxygen, so it can save life if blown into a casualty's lungs (artificial ventilation). If circulation is absent, this is combined with chest compressions (cardio-pulmonary resuscitation or CPR, *see page 16*), so that oxygen reaches vital organs.

> **USING FACE SHIELDS**
> Artificial ventilation carries little risk of the transfer of infection. First Aiders, however, may be trained to use a shield for hygienic reasons. If you are trained to use one, carry it at all times. If without one, do not hesitate to give ventilations.

GIVING MOUTH-TO-MOUTH VENTILATION

1 Keep the airway open with two fingers under the chin and a hand on the forehead (*see page 11*).

2 Remove *obvious* obstructions, such as broken or displaced dentures. Leave well-fitting dentures in place.

3 Close the nose by pinching it with your index finger and thumb. Take a full breath and place your lips around his mouth, making a seal.

4 Blow into the casualty's mouth until you see the chest rise. Take about two seconds for full inflation.

5 Remove your lips. Allow the chest to fall fully, which takes about four seconds. Repeat this once. Assess for signs of circulation (*see page 16*).

Lift chin to tilt back head

Pinch nose closed

IF the circulation is absent (*see page 16*) with no pulse or signs of recovery, such as return of skin colour, swallowing, coughing, or breathing, begin cardio-pulmonary resuscitation (*see page 16*).

IF circulation is present, continue ventilations and check the pulse after every ten breaths.
IF breathing returns, place the casualty in the recovery position (*see page 12*).

IF THE CHEST DOES NOT RISE

If, after attempting two ventilations, the chest does not rise, check that:
* the head is tilted sufficiently;
* you have closed the nostrils;
* you have firmly sealed the mouth;
* the airway is not obstructed.

IF the casualty is not known to have choked, attempt three further breaths then assess for circulation (*see page 16*).

IF you know he has choked, see below.

IF YOU NEED TO CLEAR AN OBSTRUCTION

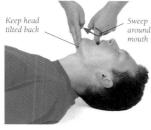

Keep head tilted back

Sweep around mouth

1 If you can see any *obvious* obstruction inside the mouth, use your finger to hook it out carefully.

DO NOT use your fingers to feel blindly down the throat.

2 Attempt three further breaths. If, after carrying out the above checks again, the chest still does not rise, treat as for unconscious choking adults (*see page 25*).

OTHER FORMS OF ARTIFICIAL VENTILATION

After rescue from water or with mouth injuries, use mouth-to-nose ventilation. It is easy to blow air in, but not easy for air to escape; the soft parts of the nose may flop back.

To give mouth-to-nose ventilation
Close the casualty's mouth. Form a seal with your lips around the nose, and blow. Open the mouth to let the breath out. For babies, use mouth-to-mouth-and-nose (*see page 21*).

Mouth-to-stoma ventilation
A laryngectomy is when the voice box (*larynx*) has been surgically removed, leaving a neck opening (*stoma*) through which breathing takes place.

Artificial ventilation is given through the stoma. If the chest fails to rise and air escapes from the mouth, he or she may be a "partial neck breather". In this case, close off the mouth and nose with your thumb and fingers.

THE RESUSCITATION SEQUENCE				
CHECK RESPONSE	OPEN AIRWAY AND CHECK BREATHING	BREATHE FOR THE CASUALTY	**ASSESS FOR CIRCULATION**	COMMENCE CPR

ASSESSING FOR CIRCULATION

Check the pulse for up to ten seconds and look for recovery signs such as return of skin colour, breathing, swallowing, and coughing.
IF you cannot find a pulse or there are no signs of circulation, begin chest compressions immediately.

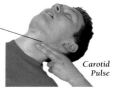

Hollow between windpipe and large neck muscle

Carotid Pulse

CARDIO-PULMONARY RESUSCITATION (CPR)

If there is no pulse, the heart has stopped and you will need to give chest compressions.

Chest compressions must always be combined with artificial ventilation, a process known as cardio-pulmonary resuscitation, or CPR for short. If both you and your helper have been trained to give CPR, you can do so together.

Calling an ambulance
♦ *If you have a helper*, send him or her to call an ambulance. Continue treating the casualty until help arrives.
♦ *If alone* with an injured or drowned casualty, resuscitate for one minute (*see page 9*) then call an ambulance. For other adult casualties, call ambulance first (*see page 9*) and then resuscitate.

GIVING CHEST COMPRESSIONS

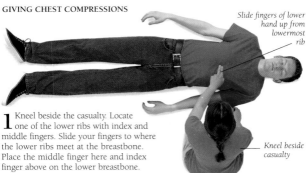

Slide fingers of lower hand up from lowermost rib

Kneel beside casualty

1 Kneel beside the casualty. Locate one of the lower ribs with index and middle fingers. Slide your fingers to where the lower ribs meet at the breastbone. Place the middle finger here and index finger above on the lower breastbone.

Slide heel of hand down to meet fingers

2 Place the heel of your other hand on the breastbone, and slide it down until it reaches your index finger. This is the point at which you should apply pressure.

Keep fingers clear of chest

3 Place the heel of your first hand on top of the other hand, and interlock your fingers.

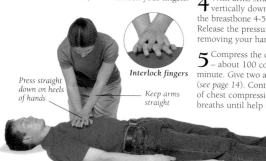

Press straight down on heels of hands

Interlock fingers

Keep arms straight

HOW CHEST COMPRESSION WORKS

Pushing down on the breastbone presses the heart against the backbone and forces blood out of the heart into the tissues. The chest then rises and more blood is "sucked" in and then forced out by the next compression.

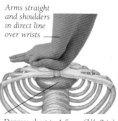

Arms straight and shoulders in direct line over wrists

Depress chest to 4-5 cm (1½-2 in)

4 With arms straight, press vertically down and depress the breastbone 4-5 cm (1½-2 in). Release the pressure without removing your hands.

5 Compress the chest 15 times – about 100 compressions a minute. Give two artificial breaths (*see page 14*). Continue this cycle of chest compressions and breaths until help arrives.

RESUSCITATION FOR CHILDREN

Respiratory failure is the main cause of cardiac arrest in a child. The resuscitation techniques used depend on the child's age and size (*see page 22*). *If he is aged eight or over*, use the adult sequence (*see page 9*).

CHECK CASUALTY'S RESPONSE
Try to get a response by talking to the child or gently shaking him (*see opposite*). If there is no response, shout for help.

OPEN *AIRWAY*; CHECK BREATHING
Tilt the head back to open the airway. Check for breathing (*see page 20*).

IF the child is breathing, place him in the recovery position (*see page 20*).

BREATHE FOR THE CASUALTY
Look into the mouth and clear any *obvious* obstruction. For a child, keep the head tilted back, pinch the nose, and give five breaths of mouth-to-mouth ventilation (*see page 21*). For a baby, keep the head tilted back and breathe into the mouth and nose (*see page 21*).

ASSESS FOR *CIRCULATION*
Check for circulation for up to ten seconds. If there is a pulse, continue with artificial ventilation (*see page 21*). If you cannot feel a pulse and there are no signs of recovery (*see page 21*), commence CPR.

COMMENCE CPR
Alternate five chest compressions with one breath of artificial ventilation (*see page 22*) for one minute (approximately 10 cycles), before calling an ambulance.

WHEN TO CALL AN AMBULANCE
IF you have a helper, he should call an ambulance while you treat the casualty.
IF alone, give one minute of CPR if circulation is absent, or one minute of ventilations if it is present, then call an ambulance. Continue treatment.

THE RESUSCITATION SEQUENCE				
CHECK RESPONSE	OPEN AIRWAY AND CHECK BREATHING	BREATHE FOR THE CASUALTY	ASSESS FOR CIRCULATION	COMMENCE CPR

CHECKING RESPONSE

BABY (UNDER ONE) AND CHILD (AGED 1–7)

Baby: Gently tap or flick the sole of his foot to see if he responds.
IF there is no response, shout for help.
Never shake a baby.
Child: Stimulate him to establish whether he is unconscious. Talk to him and gently shake him.
IF unconscious, he won't respond.
IF there is no response, shout for help.

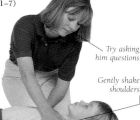

Try asking him questions

Gently shake shoulders

OPENING THE AIRWAY

BABY (UNDER ONE)

Do not over-extend neck

Use one finger to lift the chin. Place the other hand on the baby's head and tilt it back slightly.

CHILD (AGED 1–7)

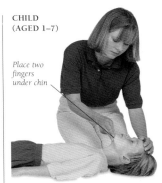

Place two fingers under chin

Use two fingers to lift the chin. Place the other hand on the child's forehead and tilt the head back.

THE RESUSCITATION SEQUENCE				
CHECK RESPONSE ▶	OPEN AIRWAY AND CHECK BREATHING ▶	**BREATHE FOR THE CASUALTY** ▶	**ASSESS FOR CIRCULATION** ▶	COMMENCE CPR

CHECKING BREATHING
FOR BOTH BABY (UNDER ONE) AND CHILD (AGED 1–7)

1 Listen for sounds of breathing; feel for breath on your cheek; and look along the chest for movement.

2 Check for up to ten seconds before deciding that breathing is absent.

Lean right down over casualty

Look for chest movement, indicating breathing

THE RECOVERY POSITION

BABY (UNDER ONE)

IF breathing and circulation are present, or return at any point during the resuscitation sequence, hold the baby in the recovery position.

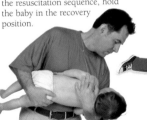

Technique for a baby
The recovery position technique for a baby is to cradle him with his head tilted downwards to stop him choking on his tongue or inhaling vomit.

CHILD (AGED 1–7)

IF breathing and circulation are present, or return at any point during the resuscitation sequence, put him in the recovery position to stop him choking on his tongue or inhaling vomit.

Bend leg to prop up body

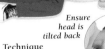

Ensure head is tilted back

Technique for a child
Place a child into the recovery position as you would an adult (*see page 12*). Open the airway before you begin turning and recheck it once the turn is complete.

BREATHING FOR THE CASUALTY

BABY (UNDER ONE YEAR)

1 Carefully remove *obvious* obstructions from the mouth. Seal your lips tightly around the baby's mouth and nose and breathe into the lungs.

Ventilate until chest rises

2 Give five breaths of mouth-to-mouth ventilation, aiming at one breath every three seconds. Check the brachial pulse (*see below*) and look for other signs of recovery, such as coughing, swallowing, or breathing.

CHILD (AGED 1–7)

1 Carefully remove any *obvious* obstruction from the mouth. Pinch the child's nostrils closed. Seal your lips around his mouth and breathe into the lungs until the chest rises.

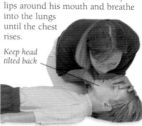

Keep head tilted back

2 Give five breaths, aiming at one breath every three seconds. Check the child's pulse and look for other signs of circulation.

FOR BOTH BABY (UNDER ONE) AND CHILD (AGED 1–7)

IF there is no circulation or other sign of recovery (*see below*), give CPR for one minute: five chest compressions (*see page 22*) for each artificial breath. Call an ambulance. Treat until help arrives.

IF circulation is present, give artificial ventilation for one minute before calling an ambulance. Treat until help arrives. IF breathing, put the baby or child in the recovery position (*see opposite*).

ASSESSING FOR CIRCULATION

Spend up to ten seconds checking the pulse. While you are doing this, look for other signs of recovery, such as

return of colour to the skin, and any signs of movement, for example breathing, swallowing, or coughing.

CHECKING THE PULSE

Baby: Feel with two fingers for the brachial pulse on the upper inside of the arm (*see right*).
Child: Check the carotid pulse in the neck (*see page 16*).

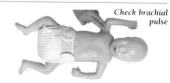

Check brachial pulse

CARDIO-PULMONARY RESUSCITATION (CPR)

If a child appears lifeless with no sign of circulation, or the pulse of an infant of less than one year is less than 60 beats a minute, begin cardio-pulmonary resuscitation (CPR). The technique depends on age and size. See below for an outline of the technique for each age group.

GUIDELINES FOR CPR ON CHILDREN

Should you have doubts about which technique to use, follow this rule: if you have to move from the chest to reach the head for mouth-to-mouth ventilations, use the adult technique (see page 9).

Age	Chest compressions	Artificial ventilations
Under one	5 (with two fingers)	1 (on mouth and nose)
1–7	5 (with one hand)	1 (on mouth only)
8 or over (treat as for an adult)	15 (with two hands)	2 (on mouth only)

BABY (UNDER ONE YEAR)

One finger's breadth below inter-nipple line

1 With the baby on her back on a flat surface, put two fingertips on the lower breastbone. Press down five times to a third of the depth of the chest at a rate of 100 a minute.

Cover baby's mouth and nose

2 Give one full breath of artificial ventilation, by breathing into the baby's mouth and nose (see page 21).

3 Alternate five chest compressions to one ventilation for a minute. Call an ambulance. Treat until help arrives.

CHILD (AGED 1–7)

1 Place your hand as for an adult (see page 16); use only one hand. Press down five times to a third of the depth of the chest at a rate of 100 a minute.

Tilt chin

2 Give one full breath of mouth-to-mouth ventilation (see page 21).

3 Alternate five chest compressions to one breath of mouth-to-mouth ventilation for one minute, then call an ambulance. Continue while waiting.

DISORDERS OF THE RESPIRATORY SYSTEM

2

Oxygen is essential to support life. The action of breathing enables air containing oxygen to be taken into the lungs, so that the oxygen can be transferred to the blood and circulated throughout the body. The action of breathing and the process of gas exchange in the lungs are together commonly described as "respiration", and the organs, tissues, and structures that enable us to breathe as the "respiratory system".

What can go wrong

Respiration can be impaired in various ways: by obstruction of the airway, for example, as in choking or drowning; by preventing normal exchange of gases in the lungs, such as in fume or smoke inhalation; or by conditions affecting the function of the lungs, for instance, as with a collapsed lung, or the mechanism of breathing, as in asthma. Disorders affecting respiration always require urgent first aid and may be life-threatening.

FIRST-AID PRIORITIES

♦ Recognise respiratory distress.

♦ Restore and maintain the casualty's breathing and, if necessary, apply the ABC of resuscitation, and be prepared to resuscitate if necessary.

♦ Identify and remove the cause of the problem, and provide fresh air.

♦ Obtain appropriate medical aid. Any casualty with severe airway or breathing difficulties must be seen at hospital, even if first aid seems to have been successful.

CHOKING

A foreign object in the throat may block it and induce choking. Adults may choke on unchewed or quickly swallowed food. Infants and babies often put objects in their mouths. Choking needs prompt first aid; be ready to resuscitate if breathing stops.

Recognition

◆ Difficulty speaking and breathing.
◆ Congested face initially.
◆ Grey-blue skin (cyanosis) later.
◆ The casualty may point to the throat, or grasp the neck.

See page 26 for Choking Baby/Child

TREATMENT

YOUR AIMS ARE:

■ To remove the obstruction and so restore normal breathing.
■ To arrange urgent removal to hospital if necessary.

CONSCIOUS ADULT

1 If the casualty is breathing, encourage her to cough, as this will help to dislodge the obstruction. Check the mouth and remove any obvious obstructions.

2 If she is weak, or stops coughing or breathing, stand to her side and slightly behind. Remove any obvious obstruction; give five sharp back slaps between the shoulders. Check the mouth.

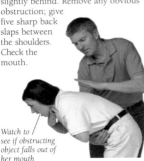

Watch to see if obstructing object falls out of her mouth

3 If the back slaps fail, stand behind the casualty. Place your arms around her abdomen, bend her slightly forwards and put your fist just below the base of the breastbone. Put your other hand on top and pull sharply inwards and upwards five times. Listen for the obstruction being dislodged. Check the mouth.

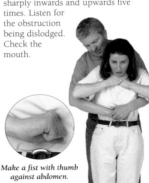

Make a fist with thumb against abdomen.

4 Repeat steps 2 and 3 three times. If the obstruction does not clear, ☎ *DIAL 999 FOR AN AMBULANCE.* Continue the cycle until help arrives.

IF the casualty becomes unconscious, or is found unconscious after choking, treat as described opposite.

ADULT WHO BECOMES UNCONSCIOUS

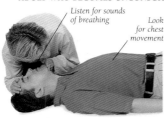

Listen for sounds of breathing

Look for chest movement

Support head and angle towards floor

1 Open the airway and check breathing (*see page 11*).
☎ *DIAL 999 FOR AN AMBULANCE.* Remove obvious obstructions. If there is no breathing, give five ventilations.

IF unsuccessful, go on to step 2, right.

2 Turn the casualty on to his side and give up to five sharp back slaps with the flat of your hand between his shoulder blades. Check his mouth and remove any obvious obstructions.

IF unsuccessful, proceed to step 3.

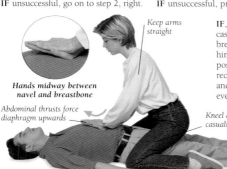

Keep arms straight

Hands midway between navel and breastbone

Abdominal thrusts force diaphragm upwards

Kneel astride casualty's thighs

IF, at any stage, the casualty begins to breathe normally, place him in the recovery position. Monitor and record breathing, pulse, and level of response every ten minutes.

3 Turn the casualty on to his back. Kneel by him or straddle him. Put the heel of a hand below his breastbone and cover it with the other hand. Press in and upwards five times. Check mouth; remove obvious obstructions.

4 If the casualty is still not breathing, try another five artificial ventilations (*see page 14*). Continue backslaps, abdominal thrusts, mouth checks, and ventilation attempts until the ambulance arrives or the casualty starts breathing.

CHOKING (CONTINUED)

CONSCIOUS BABY (0–12 MONTHS)

1 If a baby is distressed, weak or stops coughing or breathing, lay him face down on your arm with his head low. Support his back and chin. Give up to five sharp back slaps between the shoulders. Check the mouth; remove any obvious obstructions with a finger. Do not feel blindly down his throat.

Push down on the breastbone one finger's breadth below nipple line with fingertips

2 If this fails, turn the baby on to his back. Use two fingers to give up to five chest thrusts. These are more vigorous than compressions. Give one every three seconds. Check the mouth.

> **DO NOT** use abdominal thrusts.

3 If the obstruction still has not cleared, repeat steps 1–3 three times, then take the baby with you to
☎ *DIAL 999 FOR AN AMBULANCE.*
Repeat steps 1–3 until help arrives.

FOR A BABY (0–12 MONTHS) WHO BECOMES UNCONSCIOUS

Open the airway and check breathing (*see pages 18–22*).
☎ *DIAL 999 FOR AN AMBULANCE.*
Carefully remove obstructions from the mouth. Attempt up to five ventilations. Give back slaps, chest thrusts, mouth checks, and ventilation attempts until help arrives or breathing resumes.

CONSCIOUS CHILD (1–7 YEARS)

1 If breathing, encourage the child to cough to dislodge the obstruction.

2 If the child seems weak, or stops coughing or breathing, stand beside him, bend him forwards and give him five sharp back slaps between the shoulder blades. Check his mouth.

3 If this fails, stand behind him. Place a fist against his lower breastbone. Grasp the fist with your other hand. Give up to five chest thrusts pressing sharply in with your fist at a rate of one every three seconds. Check the mouth.

4 If the chest thrusts fail, make a fist against the central upper abdomen. Grasp the fist with your other hand. Press into his abdomen with a sharp upward thrust up to five times. Check mouth.

Fist between breastbone and navel

5 If the abdominal thrusts fail, repeat steps 2-4 three times.

IF unsuccessful, proceed to step 6.

6 ☎ *DIAL 999 FOR AN AMBULANCE.* Continue the cycle until help arrives.

IF the child becomes unconscious, treat him as described opposite.

CHILD (1–7 YEARS) WHO BECOMES UNCONSCIOUS

1 Open the airway and check breathing.
☎ **DIAL 999 FOR AN AMBULANCE.**
Remove any obvious obstruction from the mouth.

> **DO NOT** use your fingers to feel blindly down the throat.

Use heel of one hand only

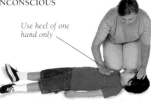

2 If the child is not breathing, attempt up to five mouth-to-mouth ventilations (*see page 21*). If this is not successful, proceed to step 3.

Use flat of your hand

Support her head

3 Turn the child on to her side and give up to five back slaps between the shoulder blades. Check the mouth. Carefully remove any obvious obstruction with one finger. If this is unsuccesful, proceed to step 4.

4 Turn the child on to her back and kneel by her side. Give up to five sharp inward (chest) thrusts on her lower breastbone. Press the chest to a third of its depth at a rate of once every three seconds.
Check the mouth.

Push upwards on central upper abdomen

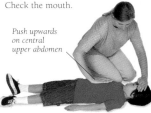

5 If chest thrusts fail, kneel by the child or straddle her. Place the heel of your hand midway between the navel and breastbone. Give up to five upward (abdominal) thrusts. Check mouth. Try another five ventilations.

6 If the obstruction has not cleared, continue back slaps, chest and abdominal thrusts, mouth checks and artificial ventilation until help arrives or the casualty resumes breathing.

IF breathing resumes, put her in the recovery position (*see page 20*).

DROWNING

Death by drowning normally occurs when water gets into the lungs instead of air. Drowning may also be caused by throat spasm.

The water that gushes out of a rescued casualty's mouth is from the stomach, and should drain naturally. Attempts to force water from the stomach may result in stomach contents being inhaled. A nearly drowned casualty should always get medical attention. Water in the lungs causes irritation and the air passages may swell hours later (secondary drowning). The casualty may also need treating for hypothermia.
See also:
Hypothermia, *page 95.*

TREATMENT

YOUR AIMS ARE:
■ To restore adequate breathing.
■ To keep the casualty warm.
■ To arrange removal to hospital.

1 If carrying the casualty from the water to safety, keep her head lower than the rest of the body to reduce the risk of inhaling water.

Tilt head to listen for breathing

2 Lay her down on her back on a coat or rug. Open the airway and check breathing; be prepared to resuscitate if necessary (*see pages 8–22*).

IF resuscitating, be aware that water in the lungs and the effects of cold can increase resistance to artificial ventilation and chest compression, so you may have to do both at a slower rate than normal.

DO NOT use the abdominal thrust unless the airway is obstructed and artificial ventilation has failed.

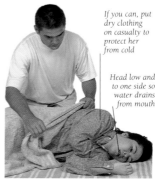

If you can, put dry clothing on casualty to protect her from cold

Head low and to one side so water drains from mouth

3 Treat the casualty for hypothermia: remove wet clothing and protect her from cold. Place her in the recovery position (*see page 12*). If she regains full consciousness, give her hot drinks.

4 ☎ *DIAL 999 FOR AN AMBULANCE,* even if she appears to recover fully.

BREATHING DIFFICULTIES

These may be caused by chronic illness, respiratory infections, or allergic reactions – respiratory or generalised. Laboured breathing can also occur in conditions not directly related to the respiratory system. Breathless attacks may result from asthma or psychological stress (*hyperventilation*). Prompt first aid can do much to help a casualty's breathing, and ease distress.

See also:
Anaphylactic Shock, *page 35.*

COLLAPSED LUNG

If air enters the space between a lung and chest wall, it may affect breathing and cause all or part of the lung to collapse (*pneumothorax*). This is caused by a lung weakness or chest injury. If under pressure, it can affect the action of the sound lung and heart. This is *life-threatening*.

If you suspect a collapsed lung, help the casualty into the position in which he can breathe most easily; call an ambulance without delay.

HYPERVENTILATION

Excessive breathing (*hyperventilation*) is often caused by acute anxiety and may accompany hysteria or a panic attack. It may be seen in susceptible people who have recently had a shock.

Excessive breathing reduces carbon dioxide levels, causing the symptoms of this condition. As normal breathing returns, the casualty will recover.

Recognition
- Unnaturally fast, deep breathing.

There may also be:
- Attention-seeking behaviour.
- Dizziness, faintness, trembling, or marked tingling in the hands.
- Cramps in the hands and feet.

TREATMENT

YOUR AIM IS:
- To remove the casualty from any cause of distress and calm him down.

1 When speaking to the casualty, be firm, but kind.

2 If possible, lead the casualty away to a quiet place, where he may be better able to calm down and regain control of his breathing.

IF this is a symptom of underlying anxiety, advise him to see his doctor.

3 If cramps persist, let him re-breathe his own exhaled air, which contains carbon dioxide, from a paper bag.

ASTHMA

This is when the air passage muscles go into spasm and the airway lining swells. The airway then narrows and breathing becomes difficult.

There may be a trigger, such as an allergy, cold, or smoke. Many sufferers are prone to sudden attacks at night.

Many asthmatics carry "relieving" inhalers, most of which have blue caps. Some carry inhalers with brown or white caps to prevent attacks. The drugs in the inhalers dilate the air passages to ease breathing.

Recognition
- Difficulty in breathing, with a very prolonged breathing-out phase.
- Wheezing as casualty breathes out.
- Distress and anxiety.
- Difficulty in speaking and whispering.
- Grey-blue skin (cyanosis).
- Dry, tickly cough.
- In a severe attack, the casualty may become exhausted. Rarely, he or she may become unconscious and stop breathing.

TREATMENT

YOUR AIMS ARE:
- To ease breathing.
- To seek medical aid if necessary.

1 Keep calm and reassure the casualty. Asthma can be frightening but a reliever inhaler usually works within a few minutes.

Fit a spacer to a child's inhaler, if she has one

2 Let her adopt the position that she finds most comfortable, which is often sitting down. Ask her to breathe slowly and deeply; this may help.

DO NOT make the casualty lie down.
DO NOT try to use a preventer inhaler to help an asthma attack.

IF the attack is mild and eases within 5–10 minutes, ask the casualty to take another dose from the same inhaler. Immediate medical help is not vital, but she should tell her doctor of the attack.

IF this is the first attack, or if it is severe, and
- the inhaler has no effect after 5–10 minutes; • the casualty is getting worse; • breathlessness makes talking difficult; • she is getting exhausted;
☎ *DIAL 999 FOR AN AMBULANCE.*
Help her to take her inhaler every 5–10 minutes. Record her breathing and pulse every ten minutes.

IF the casualty stops breathing or loses consciousness, open the airway and check breathing; be ready to resuscitate if necessary (*see pages 8–22*).
☎ *DIAL 999 FOR AN AMBULANCE.*

DISORArchive OF THE CIRCULATION

DISORDERS OF THE CIRCULATION

3

The heart and network of blood vessels, that are together known as the circulatory (or cardiovascular) system, work constantly to keep all parts of the body supplied with blood, which carries vital oxygen and nutrients.

The circulatory system can fail for two main reasons: severe bleeding and fluid loss may cause the volume of circulating blood to fall, and deprive the vital organs, primarily the brain, heart, and lungs, of oxygen; and secondly, age or disease can cause the body's circulatory system to break down.

First-aid techniques

The techniques described in this chapter demonstrate how to improve the blood supply to the heart and brain. In minor incidents, for example, when a casualty faints, appropriate first aid should ensure recovery; in serious cases, such as heart attack, your role may be vital in preserving life until medical aid arrives.

FIRST-AID PRIORITIES

◆ Position casualty to improve blood supply to the vital organs.

◆ Improve circulation and breathing – for example, loosening any tight clothing.

◆ Comfort and reassure the casualty.

◆ Advise the casualty to inform his doctor of an unexplained faint or angina attack; call an ambulance if you suspect an emergency.

SHOCK

The circulatory system sends blood round the body, so that oxygen and nutrients can pass through to the tissues. If the system fails, circulatory shock develops. If this is not treated swiftly, vital organs may fail, leading to death. The condition can be made worse by fear and pain.

Where there is a risk of shock, reassuring the casualty and making him comfortable may prevent the condition deteriorating. Do not confuse circulatory shock with psychogenic shock, which occurs when, for example, a person suffers deep emotional stress.

What causes circulatory shock?

Shock can develop if the heart fails to pump blood through the body, or if blood vessels dilate, as in severe infection or anaphylactic shock, reducing the blood pressure.

Shock may also occur if the blood supply to the organs is reduced through blood loss or loss of other bodily fluids through burns, severe diarrhoea, or vomiting. The body responds initially by diverting blood from the surface to the organs. Shock develops if fluid loss is not stopped.

Recognition

At first, adrenaline causes:
◆ A rapid pulse. ◆ Pale, grey-blue skin, especially inside lips. A pressed nail or earlobe will not regain colour immediately.
◆ Sweating, and cold, clammy skin.

As shock develops, there may be:
◆ Weakness and giddiness. ◆ Nausea, and possibly vomiting. ◆ Thirst.
◆ Rapid, shallow breathing.
◆ A weak, "thready" pulse.

As the brain's oxygen supply weakens:
◆ The casualty is restless, anxious, and even aggressive.
◆ The casualty may yawn and gasp for air. ◆ Consciousness is lost.
◆ Finally, the heart will stop.

See also:

Severe Burns and Scalds, *page 86*
Severe External Bleeding, *page 40*.

THE BODY'S REACTION TO BLOOD LOSS	
Approximate volume	*Effect on the body*
0.5 litre (1 pint)	Little or no effect; this is the quantity normally taken in a blood-donor session.
2 litres (3½ pints)	Hormones are released that quicken the pulse, and induce sweating. Small blood vessels in non-vital areas, such as the skin, shut down to divert blood and oxygen to the vital organs. Shock is evident.
3 litres (5 pints)	As blood or fluid loss approaches this level (half the normal volume of the average adult), the pulse at the wrist may be undetectable. Consciousness is lost; breathing and heart may fail.

TREATMENT

YOUR AIMS ARE:
- To recognise shock.
- To treat any obvious cause.
- To improve the blood supply to the brain, heart, and lungs.
- To arrange removal to hospital.

DO NOT let the casualty smoke, eat, drink, or move unnecessarily. If she complains of thirst, moisten her lips with a little water.

DO NOT leave casualty alone.

1 Treat any cause of shock you identify (such as external bleeding).

2 Lay the casualty down on a blanket to protect her from the cold ground, keeping her head low. Constantly reassure the casualty.

Put cushion on chair to make it more comfortable

Prop up legs as high as possible

Keeping head low may prevent casualty losing consciousness

3 Raise and support her legs to improve the blood supply to the vital organs. Take care if you suspect a fracture.

DO NOT try to warm casualty with a hot-water bottle or any other direct source of heat.

4 Loosen tight clothing, such as braces or belts, to reduce constriction at the neck, chest, and waist.

Protect casualty from cold with coats or blankets

Check breathing, pulse, and level of response at regular intervals

5 Keep the casualty warm by covering her with coats or blankets.
☎ **DIAL 999 FOR AN AMBULANCE.**

6 Check and record breathing, pulse, and level of response. Be ready to resuscitate if necessary (see pages 8–22).

FAINTING

A faint (also known as *syncope*) is a brief loss of consciousness that is caused by a temporary reduction of blood flow to the brain. Unlike shock (*see page 32*), the pulse becomes very slow, although it soon returns to normal. Recovery from a faint is usually rapid and complete.

A faint may be caused by pain or fright, upset, exhaustion, or lack of food. It is more common, however, after long periods of inactivity, especially in a warm atmosphere.

This causes blood to pool in the lower body, reducing the amount of oxygen available to the brain.

Recognition
◆ A brief loss of consciousness causing casualty to fall to the floor.
◆ A slow pulse.
◆ Pale, cold skin and sweating.

TREATMENT

YOUR AIMS ARE:
■ To improve blood flow to the brain.
■ To reassure the casualty as she recovers, and make her comfortable.

Support her ankles on your shoulders

Watch her face for signs of recovery

Raise legs to improve blood flow to brain

1 Lay the casualty down, and raise and support her legs.

2 Make sure she has plenty of fresh air; open a window if necessary.

3 As she recovers, reassure her and help her sit up gradually.

4 Look for and treat any injury that has been sustained through falling.

IF she does not regain consciousness quickly, open the airway and check breathing; be ready to resuscitate if necessary (*see pages 8–22*). Place her in the recovery position (*see page 12*).
☎ *DIAL 999 FOR AN AMBULANCE.*

IF she starts to feel faint again, tell her to lie down, and raise and support her legs until she recovers fully.

ANAPHYLACTIC SHOCK

This is a potentially fatal major allergic reaction. It may develop in susceptible individuals within seconds or minutes of, for example,
◆ the injection of a specific drug;
◆ the sting of a certain insect;
◆ the ingestion of a particular food, such as peanuts.

Chemical substances are released that dilate blood vessels and constrict air passages. Blood pressure falls dramatically and breathing is impeded. The face and neck can swell, increasing the risk of suffocation. Oxygen to the vital organs (heart, brain, and lungs) is severely reduced. A casualty with anaphylactic shock urgently needs oxygen and a life-saving injection of adrenaline. First aid is limited to assisting breathing and minimising shock until specialised help arrives.

Recognition
◆ Anxiety. ◆ Widespread red, blotchy skin rash.
◆ Swelling of the face and neck.
◆ Puffiness around the eyes.
◆ Impaired breathing, from a tight chest to severe difficulty; the casualty may wheeze and gasp for air.
◆ A rapid pulse.

TREATMENT

YOUR AIM IS:
■ To arrange urgent removal to hospital.

1 ☎ *DIAL 999 FOR AN AMBULANCE.* Give any information you have on the cause of the casualty's condition.

2 Help a conscious casualty sit up in the position that most relieves any breathing difficulty.

Sitting helps breathing

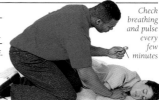

Check breathing and pulse every few minutes

Insulate casualty from cold with blanket or coat

IF she becomes unconscious, open the airway, check breathing and be ready to resuscitate (*see pages 8–22*). Put her in the recovery position (*see page 12*).

Some who are aware of their allergy have an adrenaline syringe (Epi-Pen). If necessary, help the casualty use it or, if trained, give it yourself.

DISORDERS OF THE HEART

The heart is a specialised pump. Its muscle, the *myocardium*, "beats" throughout our lives in a smooth, continuous, and co-ordinated way, controlled by an electrical impulse. The heart muscle has its own blood supply, provided by the coronary arteries (so-called because they encircle the heart like a crown). Like all other arteries, the coronary ones are susceptible to narrowing and blockage, which can impede or prevent the oxygen from reaching the heart muscle. If severe, or if the electrical impulse is disrupted, the heart may stop (*cardiac arrest*).

ANGINA PECTORIS

The name means a constriction of the chest, and describes the pain that a person experiences when narrowed coronary arteries are unable to deliver sufficient blood to the heart muscle to meet the demands of exertion or, sometimes, of excitement. An attack forces the casualty to rest; the pain should then soon ease.

Recognition
- Gripping central chest pain, spreading often to the jaw and down the left arm.
- Shortness of breath.
- Weakness, often sudden and extreme.
- Feeling of anxiety.

TREATMENT

YOUR AIMS ARE:
- To ease strain on the heart by ensuring that the casualty rests.
- To obtain medical help if necessary.

1 Help the casualty to sit down. Make her comfortable and reassure her.

2 If casualty has medicine for angina, such as tablets or a "puffer", let her administer it; help her, if necessary.

3 Encourage the casualty to rest and keep bystanders away. The attack should ease within a few minutes.

IF the pain persists or returns, suspect a heart attack.

☎ *DIAL 999 FOR AN AMBULANCE.*

Casualty with angina may have "puffer" to ease attack

4 Record her breathing and pulse rates every ten minutes, and be ready to resuscitate if necessary (*see* pages 8–22).

HEART ATTACK

A heart attack usually occurs when the blood supply to part of the heart muscle is blocked, for example, by a clot in a coronary artery. The main risk is that the heart will stop. The effect of an attack depends on how much heart muscle is affected; many casualties recover completely.

Drugs that aid recovery include *thrombolytics*, which dissolve the clot, and aspirin, which "thins" blood.
See also: Cardiac Arrest, *page 38*.

Recognition

◆ Persistent, vice-like central chest pain, spreading often to the jaw and the left arm. The pain does not ease during rest, and may occur at rest.
◆ Breathlessness, and discomfort in the abdomen, like severe indigestion.
◆ Sudden faintness or giddiness.
◆ A sense of impending doom.
◆ "Ashen" skin; blueness at the lips.
◆ A rapid, weak, or irregular pulse.
◆ Collapse, often with no warning.

TREATMENT

YOUR AIMS ARE:
■ To minimise the work of the heart.
■ To summon urgent medical help and arrange removal to hospital.

1 Make the casualty as comfortable as possible to ease the strain on his heart. A half-sitting position, with the casualty's head and shoulders well supported and his knees bent, is often best.

Help him into a comfortable position

2 ☎ *DIAL 999 FOR AN AMBULANCE.* State that you suspect a heart attack. If the casualty asks you to do so, call his own doctor as well.

3 Record breathing and pulse rates, and be ready to resuscitate if necessary (*see pages 8–22*).

4 If the casualty has medicine for angina, such as tablets or a "puffer" aerosol, help him to take it. If the pain persists, and the casualty is fully conscious, give him a full dose (300mg) aspirin tablet to chew.

ACUTE HEART FAILURE
Heart failure occurs when the heart muscle is strained, for example, following coronary thrombosis. Acute attacks often occur at night and may resemble asthma (*see page 30*), with breathlessness, often accompanied by other signs of heart attack. Treat as for Heart Attack, above.

CARDIAC ARREST

"Cardiac arrest" means sudden heart stoppage. There are many reasons for an arrest, including heart attack (*see page 37*), severe blood loss (*see page 40*), anaphylactic shock (*see page 35*), or hypothermia (*see page 95*). An arrest is characterised by absence of pulse and breathing. Resuscitate at once as without oxygen supplied by the blood, the heart muscle and brain cells will deteriorate rapidly. The ABC of resuscitation is fully described in the chapter on Resuscitation (*see pages 8–22*).

Recognition

- Absence of pulse.
- Absence of breathing.

TREATMENT

YOUR AIMS ARE:

- To arrange urgent removal to hospital.
- To keep the heart muscle and brain supplied with oxygen until help arrives.

Check the level of consciousness, and breathing and pulse rates.
☎ *DIAL 999 FOR AN AMBULANCE.*
IF breathing and pulse are absent, begin CPR (*see pages 16 and 22*).

VENTRICULAR FIBRILLATION

This most common cause of cardiac arrest is an electric storm originating in a chamber of the heart (ventricle) that has been damaged or deprived of oxygen. The electrical impulse of the heart becomes chaotic, and the heart muscle fails to contract in harmony.

The use of defibrillators
Ventricular fibrillation is often reversed by the early application of a controlled electric shock from a defibrillator machine, which is now carried by most ambulances. Your task as the First Aider is to keep the brain supplied with oxygen by cardiopulmonary resuscitation (*see pages 14–22*) until a defibrillator can be brought to the casualty and used by a *trained operator.*

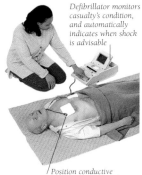

Defibrillator monitors casualty's condition, and automatically indicates when shock is advisable

Position conductive pads one each side of heart

NEVER deliver a shock to a casualty who has a pulse.

WOUNDS AND BLEEDING

4

A ny abnormal break in the skin or body surface is a wound. Open wounds allow blood and fluids to be lost from the body and germs to enter. If the bleeding is internal, the wound is closed. This is most easily recognised by bruising, indicating damage to blood vessels beneath the skin.

Wounds can be daunting, particularly if there is a lot of bleeding, but prompt action reduces blood loss and shock.

Understanding treatment procedures

This chapter shows the effect on the body of the various types of bleeding and gives treatments for major, internal, and minor wounds. It is important to guard against cross-infection while treating a wound. If possible, use latex gloves.

FIRST-AID PRIORITIES

- Control blood loss by applying pressure over the wound and raising the injured part.

- Take steps to minimise shock, which can result from severe blood loss.

- Cover any open wound with a dressing, to protect it from infection and promote healing.

- Pay scrupulous attention to hygiene, so that there is no spread of infection between the casualty and yourself.

SEVERE EXTERNAL BLEEDING

Dramatic external bleeding can be distressing, and may distract you from first-aid priorities; remember the ABC of resuscitation (see page 8). Bleeding at the face or neck can impede the airway. It is rare for bleeding to cause the heart to stop; however, shock may develop and the casualty may lose consciousness.

See also:
Shock, page 32.

PROTECTING YOURSELF
Try to use disposable gloves. Wash hands well before, and after, treatment. Cover sores or open wounds with a waterproof adhesive dressing.

TREATMENT

YOUR AIMS ARE:
- To control the bleeding.
- To prevent and minimise shock.
- To minimise the risk of infection.
- To arrange urgent removal of the casualty to hospital.

1 Remove or cut clothing to expose the wound. Watch out for sharp objects, like glass, that may injure you.

Squeeze wound edges together around object

IF you cannot apply direct pressure, for example, if an object is protruding, press down firmly on either side.

Press for ten minutes to give blood time to clot

2 Apply direct pressure over the wound with your fingers or palm, preferably over a sterile dressing or clean pad – but do not waste time hunting for a dressing.

Elevate injured part to slow blood flow to area

3 Raise and support an injured limb above the level of the casualty's heart. Handle the limb very gently if there is a fracture (see page 64).

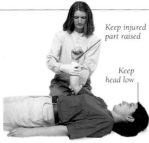

Keep injured part raised

Keep head low

4 Lay the casualty down. This will reduce blood flow to the site of injury, and minimise shock.

5 Leaving any original pad in place, apply a sterile dressing. Bandage it in place firmly, but not so tightly as to impede the circulation. If bleeding seeps through the dressing, bandage another firmly over the top.

Bandage over pads, not foreign body

Spare rolled bandages make good padding

IF there is a protruding foreign body, build up padding on either side of the object until high enough to bandage over the object without pressing on it.

6 Secure and support the injured part with bandaging (*see page 65*).

7 ☎ *DIAL 999 FOR AN AMBULANCE.* Treat the casualty for shock. Check the circulation beyond the bandage.

INDIRECT PRESSURE

If direct pressure is difficult, or fails to stop bleeding, you can apply "indirect pressure" above an artery, near the bone. Find the artery by feeling for a pulse (*see below*). Apply pressure until blood supply is reduced; do not apply longer than 10 minutes unless a femoral artery.

> **DO NOT** apply a tourniquet; it can worsen bleeding, and may cause tissue damage or gangrene.

Brachial pressure point
The brachial artery runs along the inner side of the upper arm. Press your fingertips in beneath the biceps muscle to feel for pulsation, and press the artery firmly against the bone.

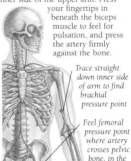

Trace straight down inner side of arm to find brachial pressure point

Feel femoral pressure point where artery crosses pelvic bone, in the groin crease

Femoral pressure point
Lay the casualty down with the knee bent to locate the groin or trouser fold, feel for the artery, then press firmly with your thumbs.

BLEEDING AT SPECIAL SITES

There are a number of wounds that require slight variations on the general rules of direct and indirect pressure if they are to be successfully treated. Blood loss from wounds at these special sites may be copious, and the casualty must be observed carefully for signs of shock.

SCALP AND HEAD WOUNDS

The scalp has a rich blood supply, and when it is damaged, the skin splits, producing a gaping wound. Bleeding may be profuse, and will often make the injury appear worse than it is. However, a scalp wound may be part of a more serious underlying injury, such as a skull fracture; examine the casualty very carefully, particularly if he or she is elderly, or when it is possible that a serious head injury is masked by alcohol or drug intoxication. If in doubt, follow the treatment for head injury.

See also:
Head Injuries, *page 52.*
Shock, *page 32.*

TREATMENT

YOUR AIMS ARE:
- To control blood loss.
- To arrange transport to hospital.

1 Wearing disposable gloves, if possible, replace any displaced skin flaps.

Pad larger than wound

Firm, steady pressure brings bleeding under control

2 Apply firm direct pressure over a sterile dressing or clean pad.

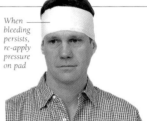

When bleeding persists, re-apply pressure on pad

3 Secure the dressing with a roller bandage. Lay the casualty down with head and shoulders slightly raised.

IF he becomes unconscious, open the airway, check breathing, and be ready to resuscitate if needed (*see pages 8–22*). Place in recovery position.

4 Take or send the casualty to hospital in final treatment position.

WOUNDS TO THE PALM

The palm is richly supplied with blood, and a wound to the palm may bleed profusely. A deep wound may also sever tendons and nerves, and result in loss of feeling in the casualty's fingers. If a foreign body prevents fist-clenching, treat as described on page 50.

TREATMENT

YOUR AIMS ARE:
- To control blood loss.
- To arrange transport to hospital.

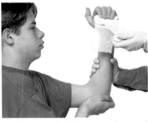

1 Press a sterile dressing or clean pad firmly into the palm and ask the casualty to clench his fist over it. If he finds it difficult to press hard, he may grasp the fist with his uninjured hand.

Bandage over top of bent fingers

Raise and support arm

2 Bandage the casualty's fingers so that they are clenched over the pad. Tie the knot over his fingers.

3 Support the casualty's arm in an elevation sling (*see page 124*), and arrange to take or send him to hospital.

WOUNDS AT JOINT CREASES

Major blood vessels cross the inside of the elbow and knee and, if severed, bleed copiously. The technique described below will, by compressing the artery, impede the blood supply to the lower part of the limb.

TREATMENT

YOUR AIMS ARE:
- To control blood loss.
- To arrange transport to hospital.

1 Press a clean pad over the injury. Bend the joint as firmly as possible.

2 Firmly bend the joint to press on the pad; raise the limb. If possible, lay casualty down to reduce shock.

3 Get the casualty to hospital. Briefly release pressure every ten minutes to restore normal blood flow.

MAJOR WOUNDS

Many wounds cause serious internal injury without severe external bleeding. This applies particularly to wounds to the trunk; a stab wound to the abdomen, for example, may produce only a small, neat entry wound, yet cause massive internal damage that needs urgent treatment.

ABDOMINAL WOUNDS

A wound's severity may be evident in bleeding and protruding abdominal contents; or there is internal injury. A stab wound, gunshot, or crushing injury may puncture, rupture or lacerate organs and blood vessels. The risk of infection and shock is high.
See also:
Internal Bleeding, page 47.
Shock, page 32.

TREATMENT

YOUR AIMS ARE:
■ To minimise the risk of infection.
■ To minimise shock.
■ To arrange urgent removal to hospital.

If wound cuts across abdomen, raise and support casualty's knees to ease strain on injury

IF the wound is vertical, do not raise the knees.

1 Lay the casualty down on a firm surface. Loosen any tight clothing.

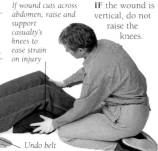

Undo belt

2 Put a large dressing over the wound, and secure it lightly with a bandage, or adhesive tape.

IF blood seeps through the dressing, add another dressing or pad on top.

IF the casualty coughs or vomits, press on the dressing to stop abdominal contents being exposed.

IF part of the intestine is protruding, do not touch it; cover it with a plastic bag or kitchen film to stop it drying out. Alternatively, use a sterile dressing.

3 ☎ *DIAL 999 FOR AN AMBULANCE.* Treat for shock. Check condition every few minutes until help arrives.

IF he becomes unconscious, open airway and check breathing; be ready to resuscitate (*see pages 8–22*). Put him in recovery position; support abdomen.

CHEST WOUNDS

The heart, lungs, and nearby blood vessels lie in the chest, protected by the breastbone and the ribcage. The ribcage also protects upper abdominal organs.

A chest wound can cause internal damage to organs in the upper abdomen. The lungs are vulnerable to injury, directly, or because their outer membranes are perforated. Air can enter between the membranes, exert pressure on the lung, and cause it to collapse: *pneumothorax*. Pressure build-up can also affect the uninjured lung and cause increased breathlessness, or

dyspnoea. When the pressure affects the heart, impairs circulation, and causes shock, there is a "*tension pneumothorax*".

Recognition

◆ Difficult, painful breathing. ◆ Alarm. *There may also be:* ◆ Shock. ◆ Coughed-up, frothy, blood. ◆ Grey-blue colour of mouth, nails, and skin. ◆ A crackling feeling of skin around wound. ◆ Blood bubbling out of wound. ◆ The sound of air being sucked into the chest. *See also:*
Shock, page 32.

TREATMENT

YOUR AIMS ARE:
■ To seal wound; maintain breathing.
■ To minimise shock.
■ To arrange urgent removal to hospital.

1 Immediately use the palm of your hand or, if the casualty is conscious, his own hand, to cover the wound.

Leave fourth side untaped to allow air to escape

Cover wound to keep clean

2 Put a sterile dressing over wound. Cover with plastic bag, kitchen film, or foil. Tape on three sides, or bandage, so that the dressing is taut.

3 Provide firm support for a conscious casualty, in the position he finds most comfortable. Encourage him to lean towards the injured side.

4 ☎ *DIAL 999 FOR AN AMBULANCE.* Treat the casualty for shock if necessary (see page 32).

Keep uninjured lung uppermost

Head tilted back, supported by hand

IF he becomes unconscious, open the airway, check breathing and be ready to resuscitate (see pages 8–22). Put him in the recovery position (see page 12), lying with the uninjured side uppermost. This will help the healthy lung to work effectively.

Eye Wounds

The eye can be bruised or cut by direct blows or by sharp, chipped fragments of metal, grit, and glass. All eye injuries are potentially serious. Even superficial grazes to the surface (cornea) of the eye can lead to scarring or infection, with possible deterioration of vision.

A penetrating wound may rupture the eyeball and allow its clear fluid content to escape. Although this type of injury is very serious, it is now possible to repair eye wounds, and the sight in the eye may not be lost.

Recognition
◆ Intense pain in the eye. ◆ A visible wound. ◆ A bloodshot appearance to the eye. ◆ Partial or total loss of vision. ◆ Leakage of blood or clear fluid from wound, possibly with visible flattening of the eyeball.

TREATMENT

YOUR AIMS ARE:
■ To prevent further damage.
■ To arrange transport to hospital.

1 Lay the casualty on her back, holding her head to keep it as still as possible.

> **DO NOT** touch or attempt to remove an embedded foreign body (see page 50).

Reassure casualty to keep her calm

Keep head supported

Give her a large, soft pad

2 Tell the casualty to keep both eyes still; movement of the "good" eye will make the injured one move and cause more damage.

Support casualty's shoulders on your knees

3 Ask the casualty to hold an eyepad, or sterile dressing, over the injured eye. This discourages the casualty from moving her eye and protects the eye from infection. If it will take some time to obtain medical help, bandage the pad in place for her.

4 Take or send her to hospital in the treatment position.

Cradle head to keep it still

INTERNAL BLEEDING

Bleeding within the body cavities may follow injury, such as a fracture or penetrating wound, but can also occur spontaneously – for example, bleeding from a stomach ulcer.

Internal bleeding is serious; even if blood is not spilt, it is still lost from the circulation, and shock can develop. Accumulated blood can also exert damaging pressure on organs such as the lungs or brain.

When to suspect internal bleeding
Suspect internal bleeding if, following injury, signs of shock develop without obvious blood loss. At the site of an injury, there may be "pattern bruising" – discolouration with the pattern of clothes or crushing objects. There may be blood at body orifices, either fresh or mixed with the contents of injured organs.

Recognition
◆ Pallor. ◆ Cold, clammy skin.
◆ A rapid, weak pulse. ◆ Pain.
◆ Thirst. ◆ Confusion, restlessness, and irritability, possibly leading to collapse and unconsciousness.
◆ After injury, pattern bruising.
◆ Bleeding from orifices.
◆ Information from the casualty indicating recent injury or illness, previous similar episodes, or drug-taking for a medical condition.
See also:
Cerebral Compression, *page 54.*
Shock, *page 32.*

TREATMENT

YOUR AIMS ARE:
■ To arrange urgent removal to hospital.
■ To minimise shock.

Take pulse at wrist

IF he loses consciousness, place him in the recovery position (*see page 12*).

1 Help the casualty to lie down, and raise and support his legs. Loosen clothing at the neck, chest, and waist.

Raise and support legs

2 ☎ *DIAL 999 FOR AN AMBULANCE.* Insulate the casualty from cold. Record breathing, pulse, and level of response every ten minutes.

3 Note the type, amount, and source of any blood loss from body orifices. If possible, send a sample with the casualty to hospital.

NOSEBLEEDS

These are most common when blood vessels in the nostrils rupture, either by a blow to the nose, or as a result of sneezing, picking, or blowing the nose. Colds or 'flu make the blood vessels more fragile; nosebleeds may also occur as a result of high blood pressure.

Nosebleeds are merely unpleasant, but can be dangerous if a lot of blood is lost. If one follows a head injury, the blood may be thin and watery. This is serious, as it is a sign that cerebrospinal fluid is leaking from the brain.
See also: Head Injuries, *page 52.*

TREATMENT

YOUR AIMS ARE:
■ To control blood loss.
■ To maintain an open airway.

1 Sit the casualty down with her head held well forward.

DO NOT let her head tip back; blood may run down her throat and induce vomiting.

Pinch child's nose for her

Ask casualty to pinch fleshy part of nose

2 Ask the casualty to breathe through her mouth (this will also have a calming effect), and to pinch the fleshy part of her nose just below the bridge. Help her if necessary.

3 Tell her to try not to speak, swallow, cough, spit, or sniff, as she may disturb blood clots. Give her a clean cloth or tissue to mop up dribble.

IF the casualty is a young child, let her dribble or spit into a bowl.

4 After ten minutes, tell the casualty to release the pressure. If her nose is still bleeding, reapply the pressure for further periods of ten minutes.

IF the nosebleed persists beyond 30 minutes, take or send the casualty to hospital in the treatment position.

5 Once the bleeding is under control, and with the casualty still leaning forward, gently clean around her nose and mouth with lukewarm water.

6 Advise the casualty to rest for a few hours, and not to blow her nose, as this will disturb any clot.

MINOR WOUNDS

Prompt first aid can help nature heal small wounds and prevent infection. But you must seek medical advice:

◆ if a foreign body is embedded;

◆ if the wound is at special risk of infection (such as a dog bite, or a puncture by a dirty object);

◆ if an old wound shows signs of becoming infected.

GOOD WOUND CARE

◆ First wash your hands thoroughly.

◆ Cover your own wounds.

◆ Don't touch the wound with your fingers (if possible, use latex gloves).

◆ Don't talk, cough, or breathe over the wound or the dressing. For more details, see page 114.

MINOR EXTERNAL BLEEDING

Minor bleeding is controlled by pressure and elevation. An adhesive dressing is normally all that is necessary.

Medical aid need only be sought if the bleeding does not stop, or if the wound is at special risk of infection.

TREATMENT

YOUR AIM IS:

■ To minimise the risk of infection.

1 First, wash your own hands well in soap and warm water. If possible, put on disposable gloves.

Rinse loose foreign particles away with water

2 If the wound is dirty, clean it by rinsing lightly under running water, or use an antiseptic wipe. Pat dry with a gauze swab. Temporarily cover the wound with sterile gauze.

3 Elevate the wounded part above the level of the heart, if possible. Avoid touching the wound directly. Support the affected limb with one hand.

Keep wounded part high

Use clean gauze swab for each stroke

Wipe away from wound

4 Clean surrounding area with soap and water. Pat dry and remove the covering. Apply an adhesive dressing.

IF there is a special risk of infection, advise the casualty to see her doctor.

FOREIGN BODIES IN MINOR WOUNDS

Small pieces of glass or grit that are lying on a wound can be carefully picked off, or rinsed off with cold water before you give any treatment to the casualty. If possible, use tweezers. However, do not attempt to remove objects that are embedded in the wound; you may damage other tissue and aggravate bleeding.

See also:
Fish Hooks, *page 101.*
Splinters, *page 100.*

TREATMENT

YOUR AIMS ARE:
■ To control bleeding without pressing the object into the wound.
■ To arrange transport to hospital.

1 Control any bleeding by applying firm pressure on either side of the object, and raising the wounded part.

Lightly drape piece of gauze over wound

2 Cover the wound with gauze to minimise the risk of infection.

3 Pad around the object until you can bandage over it without pressing down. Hold the padding in place while finishing the bandaging.

IF you cannot pad high enough, bandage *around* the object.

4 Arrange to take or send the casualty to hospital.

BRUISES

These are caused by internal bleeding. Bruising can develop slowly, appearing days later. Rapid bruising benefits from first aid, although it may indicate a deeper injury. The elderly and those on anticoagulants can bruise easily.

See also:
Internal Bleeding, page 47.

TREATMENT

YOUR AIM IS:
■ To reduce blood flow to injury, and swelling, by cooling and compression.

Raise and support the injured part in a comfortable position. Apply a cold compress (*see page 119*) to the bruise.

IF you suspect more serious underlying injury, seek medical advice.

DISORDERS OF CONSCIOUSNESS

5

The nervous system is the most highly developed system within the human body: it controls consciousness, contains centres for memory, speech, thought, and will, and also correlates the activities of other body systems.

A fully conscious person is awake, alert, and aware of his or her surroundings. Sleep is a normal state of lowered consciousness, but unconsciousness is an abnormal state in which the body's control mechanisms are impaired or lost. When a person is asleep, vital functions such as breathing take place automatically. If a person is unconscious, muscle control is lost, so if the person is lying on his or her back, the tongue falls towards the back of the throat and may block the airway. An unconscious casualty will therefore require immediate first aid.

Unconsciousness and impaired consciousness

There are a number of disorders that cause varying levels of impaired or lost consciousness; after checking the casualty's airway, breathing, and pulse (*see page 16*), you must establish the level of *consciousness*.

FIRST-AID PRIORITIES

◆ Open airway and resuscitate if needed.

◆ Protect from harm.

◆ Monitor responses.

◆ Treat other injuries.

◆ If unconscious more than three minutes or condition seems serious, get casualty to hospital.

HEAD INJURIES

All head injuries are potentially dangerous and need assessing, particularly if consciousness is impaired. A scalp wound (*see page 42*) may be obvious, but deeper damage may not be. Conversely, impaired consciousness may mask other injuries: examine the casualty fully. Unconsciousness can result from a head injury, or consciousness may be lost for other reasons and the injury sustained in a fall.

CONCUSSION

The brain is free to move a little in the skull, and can be "shaken" by a violent blow. This may cause concussion, a condition of widespread but temporary disturbance of the brain. A period of unconsciousness will follow injury, but it is always brief and followed by complete recovery – by definition, concussion can only be diagnosed once the casualty has recovered.

Recognition
◆ Brief or partial loss of consciousness following a blow to the head.
There may also be:
◆ Dizziness or nausea on recovery.
◆ Loss of memory of events at the time of, or immediately preceding, the injury.
◆ A mild, generalised headache.

CONCUSSION: CAUSES

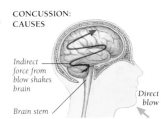

Indirect force from blow shakes brain

Direct blow

Brain stem

TREATMENT

YOUR AIMS ARE:
■ To ensure that the casualty recovers fully and safely.
■ If necessary, to seek medical aid.

1 Place an unconscious casualty in the recovery position (*see page 12*). Record breathing, pulse, and level of response every ten minutes.

IF the casualty is a child or unconscious for more than three minutes,
☎ *DIAL 999 FOR AN AMBULANCE.*

IF an adult casualty regains consciousness within three minutes, watch closely for any deterioration in the level of response, even after an apparent full recovery.

2 Put the casualty in a responsible person's care. Do not allow a casualty injured on a sports field to "play on" without a doctor's approval.

3 Advise the casualty to see his own doctor if headache, sickness, or tiredness occur after injury.

SKULL FRACTURE

A head wound may mean skull fracture; the casualty could be unconscious. A skull fracture may indicate brain damage and germs that cause infection can enter the brain. Clear fluid or watery blood leaking from the ear or nose are signs of serious injury and an entry point for germs. Suspect a skull fracture in a casualty who has received a head injury causing unconsciousness. However, if violent head movements have caused unconsciousness, there *may* also be an *associated neck injury*.

Recognition

◆ A wound or bruise on the head.
◆ A soft area or depression of the scalp. ◆ Impairment of consciousness.
◆ A progressive deterioration in the level of response. ◆ Clear fluid or watery blood coming from the nose or ear. ◆ Blood in the white of the eye.
◆ Distortion or lack of symmetry of the head or face.

See also:

Bleeding From the Scalp, *page 42*.
Diagnosis of a Skull Fracture, *page 54*.

TREATMENT

YOUR AIMS ARE:
■ To resuscitate if necessary.
■ To maintain an open airway.
■ To arrange urgent removal of the casualty to hospital.

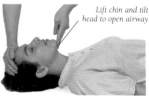

Lift chin and tilt head to open airway

1 If the casualty is unconscious, open the airway, check breathing, and be prepared to resuscitate if necessary (*see pages 8–22*). Place her in the recovery position (*see page 12*).

IF you suspect spinal injury, treat the casualty as described on pages 75–9.

2 Help a conscious casualty lie down, with head and shoulders raised.

IF there is discharge from an ear, position the casualty so that the affected ear is lower. Cover the ear with a sterile dressing or clean pad, lightly secured with a bandage. Do not plug the ear.

3 Control any bleeding from the scalp. Look for, and treat, other injuries.
☎ *DIAL 999 FOR AN AMBULANCE.*

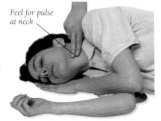

Feel for pulse at neck

4 Record breathing, pulse, and responses every ten minutes until help arrives. Make sure your notes accompany the casualty to hospital.

DIAGNOSIS OF A FRACTURE

Many skull fractures, such as linear ones, can only be diagnosed by X-ray or imaging methods. Severe injuries may cause cracking. A depressed fracture may cause bone fragments to injure or exert pressure on the brain.

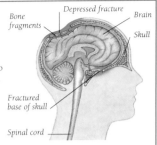

Depressed fracture

Bone fragments

Brain

Skull

Fractured base of skull

Spinal cord

Causes of a fracture

A depressed fracture is caused by a direct blow; a fracture at the skull's base may be caused by landing heavily on the feet or base of spine.

CEREBRAL COMPRESSION

This condition often needs surgery. It occurs when pressure is exerted on the brain, for example, by an accumulation of blood or by swelling of an injured brain. It is often linked to head injury and skull fracture, but can be due to causes like stroke or tumour. It can develop straight after a head injury, or be delayed for hours, or days. Always try to find out if there has been a recent head injury.

COMPRESSION CAUSED BY BLEEDING

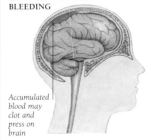

Accumulated blood may clot and press on brain

Recognition

◆ Level of response will deteriorate.
There may also be:
◆ A recent head injury, followed by an apparently full recovery. Later, the casualty may become disorientated.
◆ An intense headache.
◆ Noisy breathing, becoming slow.
◆ A slow, yet full and strong pulse.
◆ Unequal or dilated pupils.
◆ Weakness or paralysis down one side of the face or body.
◆ High temperature; flushed face.
◆ Drowsiness.
◆ A change in personality or behaviour, such as irritability.

TREATMENT

☎ *DIAL 999 FOR AN AMBULANCE.*

IF unconscious, open airway, check breathing, and be ready to resuscitate if needed (*see pages 8–22*).

IF conscious, support in comfortable position. *Record* breathing, pulse, and level of response every ten minutes.

STROKE

This term describes a condition in which the blood supply to part of the brain is suddenly and seriously impaired by a clot or ruptured artery.

Strokes are more common in later life, and in those who suffer high blood pressure or a circulatory disorder. The seriousness depends on how much, and which part, of the brain is affected. Major strokes can be fatal, but many people recover completely from minor strokes.

Recognition

◆ A sudden, severe headache.
◆ A confused, emotional mental state similar to drunkenness.
◆ Sudden or gradual loss of consciousness.
◆ Signs of weakness or paralysis, possibly on one side of the body, such as a drooping, dribbling mouth; slurred speech; loss of power or movement in the limbs; pupils of unequal size; loss of bladder or bowel control.

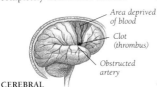

Area deprived of blood
Clot (thrombus)
Obstructed artery

CEREBRAL THROMBOSIS

Extent of bleeding
Ruptured artery

CEREBRAL HAEMORRHAGE

TREATMENT

YOUR AIMS ARE:
■ To maintain an open airway.
■ To minimise brain damage.
■ To get casualty to hospital at once.

UNCONSCIOUS CASUALTY

1 Open airway. Check breathing; be ready to resuscitate (*see pages 8–22*). Put in recovery position (*see page 12*).

2 Loosen any clothing that might impede the casualty's breathing.

3 *Record* breathing, pulse, and responses every ten minutes.

☎ *DIAL 999 FOR AN AMBULANCE.*

CONSCIOUS CASUALTY

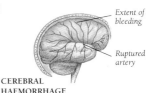

Casualty may dribble on affected side

Lay her down with head and shoulders slightly raised and supported. Incline head to one side; place a towel or cloth on her shoulder to absorb dribbling.

☎ *DIAL 999 FOR AN AMBULANCE.*

DO NOT give her food or drink.

CONVULSIONS

A convulsion, or fit, consists of involuntary muscle contractions, caused by a disturbance in the brain. Convulsions usually result in loss of, or impaired, consciousness.

There are a number of causes, including head injury, brain-damage, and lack of oxygen to the brain. In babies and young children, fits may be due to a high temperature. Fits are also a feature of *epilepsy*.

No matter what the cause of the fit, do not move the casualty unnecessarily or leave him alone; protect him from harm during a fit, and arrange appropriate aftercare.

MINOR EPILEPSY

Short of major epilepsy, there are many forms of epilepsy, including *absence seizures* which cause only a brief blurring of consciousness, like daydreaming. On recovery, the casualty may simply have lost the thread of what he or she was doing. The level of consciousness varies in all forms of minor epilepsy, but a major fit sometimes follows a minor one.

Recognition
◆ Sudden "switching off"; the casualty may be staring blankly ahead.
◆ Slight or localised twitching or jerking of the lips, eyelids, head, or limbs.
◆ Odd "automatic" movements, for example, lip-smacking, chewing, or making noises.

TREATMENT

YOUR AIM IS:
■ To protect the casualty until she is fully recovered.

1 Help the casualty to sit down in a quiet place. Remove any possible sources of harm, for example, hot drinks or sharp objects, from the immediate vicinity.

2 Talk to her calmly and reassuringly. Do not ask lots of questions. Stay with her until she is herself again.

IF the casualty does not recognise her condition, advise her to see her doctor as soon as possible.

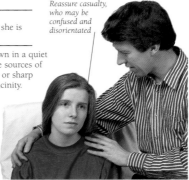

Reassure casualty, who may be confused and disorientated

MAJOR EPILEPSY

This is characterised by recurrent, major disturbances of brain activity, resulting in violent seizures (*tonic-clonic*) and severe impairment of consciousness. Epileptic fits can be sudden and dramatic, but there may be a brief warning period with, for example, an odd feeling, taste, or smell.

Recognition

An epileptic fit usually follows a pattern:
* The casualty suddenly falls unconscious, often letting out a cry.
* He becomes rigid, arching his back.
* Breathing may cease. The lips may show a grey-blue tinge (*cyanosis*) and the face and neck become congested.
* Convulsive movements begin with clenched jaw and noisy breathing. Saliva may be blood-stained if lips or tongue have been bitten. Bladder or bowel control may be lost.
* The muscles relax and breathing is normal; consciousness is recovered, usually in a few minutes. He may feel dazed, or be in a state of "automatism", unaware of his actions. A fit may also be followed by a deep sleep.
* There may be evidence of injury, such as burns or scars, from previous fits.

TREATMENT

YOUR AIMS ARE:
■ To protect the casualty from injury while the fit lasts.
■ To provide care when consciousness has been regained.

1 If you see the casualty falling, try to support him or ease his fall. Make space around him and ask bystanders to move away.

2 Loosen clothing around neck and protect head.

3 When the fit stops, put him in recovery position (*see page 12*). Check breathing; resuscitate if needed (*see pages 8–22*). Stay with him until he is fully recovered.

If possible, put something soft under or around his head

DO NOT lift or move the casualty unless he is in immediate danger.

DO NOT use force to restrain him, or put anything in his mouth.

IF he is unconscious for more than ten minutes or convulsing for more than five, is having repeated fits or his first fit, or is unaware of his condition,

☎ *DIAL 999 FOR AN AMBULANCE.*
Note the time and duration of the fit.

Loosen any tight clothing

57

CONVULSIONS IN YOUNG CHILDREN

Although young children can have epileptic fits like adults (*see page 56*) they may, more commonly, develop fits at the onset of an infectious disease, or with a throat or ear infection associated with a greatly raised body temperature or fever (*febrile convulsion*).

These convulsions can be alarming, but are rarely dangerous if properly managed. For safety's sake, the child should be seen at a hospital to eliminate a serious condition. This may be upsetting if you are the child's parent, but be reassured that, in most cases, no problems occur once the fit passes.

Recognition
◆ Fever: flushed skin, sweating.
◆ Violent muscle twitching, with clenched fists and an arched back.
◆ Twitching of the face with squinting, fixed, or upturned eyes.
◆ Breath-holding, with congested face and neck or drooling at the mouth.
◆ Loss of, or altered, consciousness.

TREATMENT

YOUR AIMS ARE:
■ To protect the child from injury.
■ To cool the child.
■ To reassure the parents.
■ To arrange removal to hospital.

Pad with pillows or rolled blankets

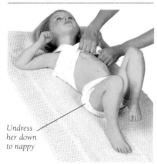

Undress her down to nappy

1 Remove any clothes or covering bedclothes. Ensure a good supply of cool, fresh air (although you should be careful not to overcool the child).

2 Position pillows or soft padding around the child so that violent movement will not result in injury.

3 Cool child by sponging with tepid water; start at her head and work down.

4 Open airway, if possible, by using recovery position (*see page 12*).

☎ *DIAL 999 FOR AN AMBULANCE.*

5 Reassure the child and parents or carer until the ambulance arrives.

OTHER DISORDERS

The nervous system may be damaged by injury and conditions like epilepsy, and also by changes in the composition of blood to the brain.

The brain is sensitive to chemical changes, such as a lack of oxygen in the blood, altered blood sugar levels, or the presence of toxins, such as poisons, alcohol, or drugs.

The problems of substance abuse
Abuse of alcohol, drugs, and other substances is an emotive subject, but never let your feelings impair management of an unconscious casualty. He is at risk from being unconscious as well as from the effects of an intoxicating substance.

The importance of examination
The symptoms of conditions such as stroke and diabetic emergency can be mistaken for intoxication. Open the airway and check breathing first, then examine the casualty to check for other causes.

DIABETES MELLITUS

This occurs when the body fails to regulate the concentration of sugar (*glucose*) in the blood. Sugar levels are normally controlled by a hormone (*insulin*) produced by the pancreas.

Without insulin, sugar builds in the blood, and can cause *hyperglycaemia* (*see below*). Diabetics must carefully balance the amount of sugar in their diet and regulate their blood sugar with insulin injections or tablets; too much insulin or too little sugar can cause *hypoglycaemia* (*see overleaf*).

Most diabetics realise the risk of hypoglycaemia if they miss a meal or over-exert themselves, and may carry sugar lumps or glucose tablets to raise their blood-sugar level quickly.

HYPERGLYCAEMIA

Prolonged high blood sugar can cause unconsciousness and diabetic coma, although a diabetic may drift into this state over a few days. This needs urgent treatment with insulin and intravenous infusion of fluids.

Recognition
♦ Dry skin and a rapid pulse.
♦ Deep, laboured breathing.
♦ A faint smell of acetone (as in nail-varnish remover) on the casualty's breath.

TREATMENT

YOUR AIM IS:
■ To arrange urgent removal of the casualty to hospital.

☎ *DIAL 999 FOR AN AMBULANCE.*
Record breathing, pulse, and level of response. Check the casualty's condition every ten minutes until the ambulance arrives.

Hypoglycaemia

When the blood-sugar level is below normal (*hypoglycaemia*), brain function is affected. This is most common with *diabetes mellitus*, but may accompany epileptic fits, follow binge drinking, and even complicate heat exhaustion and hypothermia.

Diabetics may have blood-testing kits and be ready for emergencies. An advanced attack, however, may affect consciousness.

Recognition
- A history of diabetes; the casualty may recognise the attack's onset.
- Weakness, faintness, or hunger.
- Palpitations and muscle tremors.

- Strange actions or behaviour; there may be confusion, belligerence, or even violence.
- Sweating.
- Pallor.
- Cold, clammy skin.
- A strong, bounding pulse.
- A deteriorating level of response.
- Shallow breathing.
- A warning card or bracelet (medic-alert), sugar lumps, tablets, or insulin syringe (similar to a pen).

See also:
Convulsions, *page 56*.
Heat Exhaustion, *page 97*.
Hypothermia, *page 95*.

TREATMENT

YOUR AIMS ARE:
- To raise the sugar content of the blood as quickly as possible.
- To obtain appropriate medical aid.

UNCONSCIOUS CASUALTY

Lift chin and tilt head to open airway

1 Open the airway, check breathing, and be ready to resuscitate (*see pages 8–22*). Place the casualty in recovery position (*see page 12*).

2 Record breathing, pulse, and response every ten minutes.

☎ *DIAL 999 FOR AN AMBULANCE.*

CONSCIOUS CASUALTY

Give a sugary drink, to raise sugar levels

1 Help the casualty to sit or lie down, and give her a sugary drink, sugar lumps, chocolate, or other sweet food.

2 If the casualty responds quickly, give more food or drink, and let her rest until she feels better. Tell her that she should see her doctor even if she feels fully recovered.

IF her condition does not improve, look for other causes of tremor and confusion, and treat as necessary.

BONE, JOINT, AND MUSCLE INJURIES

6

The skeleton is the framework of bones around which the body is constructed, and which supports tissues. Joints and muscles attached to the bones enable movement. Most movements are controlled at will, and co-ordinated by impulses that travel from the brain via nerves to every muscle and joint in the body.

Diagnosing types of injury

It can be hard to distinguish between bone, joint, and muscle injuries, so it helps to know how and why an injury can happen. This information is given with treatment principles for different injuries. There are first-aid treatments for injuries to bones, joints, and muscles in each part of the body.

Skull fracture, because of the effect on the brain, is discussed in the previous chapter, *Disorders of Consciousness*.

FIRST-AID PRIORITIES
◆ Maintain an open airway.

◆ Steady and support injured part, if possible.

◆ Give support, with padding, firm bandaging or splinting, ideally of an uninjured body part.

◆ If a broken bone lies in a large bulk of tissue (for example, the thigh), treat casualty for shock.

◆ Obtain appropriate medical treatment.

TYPES OF INJURY

Bones may be broken (fractured), displaced at a joint (dislocated), or both. Muscles, and the tendons that attach them to bones, may be strained or torn, and the ligaments holding the joints together can tear. If you have any doubt about which type of injury you are dealing with, it is best to opt for the most serious, which is generally a fracture.

FRACTURES

A fracture is a break or crack in a bone. Bones are not brittle like chalk, but are tough and resilient. When struck or twisted, they bend like branches. Generally, considerable force is needed to break a bone, unless it is diseased or old. Conversely, young bones that are growing are supple and may split, bend, or crack like a young sapling – hence the term "green-stick fracture".

Any fracture may be accompanied by an open wound, and complicated by injury to adjoining nerves, muscles, blood vessels, and organs.

Simple
This is a clean break or a crack in the bone.

Comminuted
This type of fracture produces multiple bone fragments.

Greenstick
A split in a young, immature bone is common in children.

OPEN AND CLOSED FRACTURES

In an open (compound) fracture, overlying skin is broken. The bone is exposed through the tissues to contamination by bacteria from the skin surface and from the air.

When the skin around a broken bone is intact, the injury is a closed fracture. There may be bruising and swelling around the fracture site.

Wound

Open
Close to the fracture, the skin is broken through which the bone may or may not protrude.

Unbroken skin

Swelling

Closed
Surrounding skin is unbroken; but internal injury to nearby tissue may cause swelling.

DISLOCATIONS

This is partial or full displacement of bones at a joint. There may be a fracture, torn ligaments (*see below*), or membrane damage. Dislocation can be caused by a force wrenching the bone, or by violent muscle contraction. This injury most often occurs to the shoulder, thumb, finger, and jaw.

A dislocated spine may injure the spinal cord, and shoulder or hip dislocation may damage nerves to the limbs and cause paralysis. A severe joint dislocation may fracture the bones involved. It can be hard to distinguish a dislocation from a fracture. Never manipulate a dislocated joint back into place; this may cause more injury.

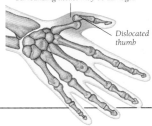

Surrounding tissues may be damaged

Dislocated thumb

SOFT TISSUE INJURIES

These injuries affect the ligaments and muscles. A *sprain* is an injury to a ligament at, or near, a joint. It is often the result of a sudden wrenching movement at the joint, that pulls the bones in the joint apart and tears the tissues surrounding the joint.

Muscles and their tendons may be overstretched and torn by violent or sudden movement. Damage to muscle tissue can occur in one of three ways.

♦ **Strain:** overstretching of the muscle, which may result in a partial tearing or pull. This often occurs at the junction of the muscle and the tendon that joins it to a bone.

♦ **Rupture:** complete tearing of the muscle, which may occur in the fleshy part or in the tendon.

♦ **Deep bruising:** may be extensive where there is a large bulk of muscle. These injuries are often accompanied by bleeding into the damaged area, causing pain, swelling, and bruising.

Athletes often suffer strains and ruptures; ligament strains and muscle tears are also common causes of non-specific back pain.

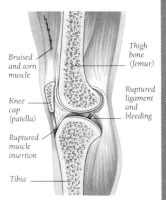

Bruised and torn muscle

Knee cap (patella)

Ruptured muscle insertion

Thigh bone (femur)

Ruptured ligament and bleeding

Tibia

TREATMENT FOR OPEN FRACTURES

YOUR AIMS ARE:
- To prevent blood loss, movement, and infection at the site of injury.
- To arrange removal to hospital, with comfortable support during transport.

> **DO NOT** move the casualty until the injured part is secured and supported, unless she is in danger.
> **DO NOT** let the casualty have anything to eat or drink.

IF you can, get a helper to support the limb while you work on the wound.

1 Cover the wound with a clean pad or sterile dressing, and apply pressure to control the bleeding (*see page 40*).

Work from uninjured side

Pad larger than wound

Secure padding with roller bandage

IF bone is protruding, build up pads of soft, non-fluffy material around the bone until you can bandage over pads.

> **DO NOT** press down directly on a protruding bone end.

Cover dressing with padding

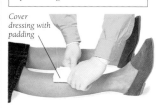

2 Without touching an open wound with your fingers, place clean padding over and around the dressing.

Secure bandage with safety pin

3 Secure the dressing and padding; bandage firmly, but not so tightly that the circulation is impeded.

4 Immobilise the injured part as for a closed fracture (*see opposite*).
☎ **DIAL 999 FOR AN AMBULANCE.**

5 Treat for shock (*see page 32*); check the circulation beyond the bandage every 10 minutes (*see page 114*).

TREATMENT FOR CLOSED FRACTURES AND DISLOCATIONS

YOUR AIMS ARE:
- To try to prevent movement at the injury site.
- To arrange removal to hospital, with comfortable support during transport.

1 Tell the casualty to keep still, and steady and support the injured part with your hands until the injury is immobilised.

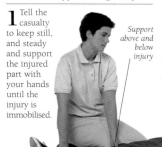

Support above and below injury

2 For firmer support, if it is not too painful, secure the injured part to a sound part of the body.
- ◆ **For upper limb fractures,** support the arm against the trunk with a sling and, if needed, bandaging (*see page 70*).
- ◆ **For lower limb fractures,** if removal to hospital is delayed, bandage sound leg to the injured one (*see page 83*).

DO NOT move the casualty until the injured part is secured and supported, unless she is in danger.
DO NOT let casualty eat or drink.
DO NOT try to replace a dislocated bone into its socket.

3 ☎ *DIAL 999 FOR AN AMBULANCE.* Treat the casualty for shock, if necessary (*see page 32*). If possible, raise the injured limb.

4 Check circulation beyond bandage every 10 minutes (*see page 114*).

TRACTION
If a fractured limb is angled so it cannot be immobilised, give gentle traction to straighten it. This overcomes the pull of muscles, and reduces pain and bleeding. Pull in the line of the bone until immobilised. Pull in a straight line; do not persist if pain is intolerable.

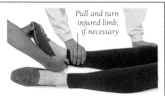

Pull and turn injured limb, if necessary

TREATMENT FOR SPRAINS AND STRAINS

Follow the "RICE" procedure (see right) to treat sprains, strains, and deep bruising initially (see page 63). If you are in doubt as to the severity of the injury, treat it as for a fracture (see page 64).

THE **RICE** PROCEDURE	
R	**R**est the injured part.
I	Apply **I**ce or a cold compress.
C	**C**ompress the injury.
E	**E**levate the injured part.

YOUR AIMS ARE:
■ To reduce swelling and pain.
■ To obtain medical aid if necessary.

1 Rest, steady, and support the injured part in the easiest position for the casualty.

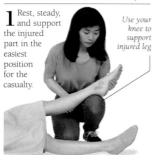

Use your knee to support injured leg

3 Apply gentle, even pressure, or compression, to the injured part by surrounding the area with a thick layer of soft padding, such as cotton wool or plastic foam, secured with a bandage.

Elevate limb

4 Raise and support the injured limb, to reduce blood flow to the injury and to minimise bruising.

2 Cool a recent injury with ice pack or cold compress (see page 119) to reduce swelling, bruising, and pain.

5 Get the casualty to hospital or, if a minor injury, advise her to rest the injury and see her doctor if necessary.

CHEEKBONE AND NOSE FRACTURES

Cheekbone and nose fractures are common – usually the result of a fight. Swelling is uncomfortable, and may block the air passages in the nose. These injuries should always be checked at hospital.

TREATMENT

YOUR AIMS ARE:
- To minimise pain and swelling.
- To arrange removal to hospital.

1 Apply a cold compress (see page 119) to reduce swelling. Treat an associated nosebleed (see page 48).

2 Arrange to take or send the casualty to hospital.

IF straw-coloured (cerebrospinal) fluid leaks from the nose, treat as for skull fracture (see page 53).

Casualty may prefer to apply compress himself

Use tea towel wrapped around bag of ice

INJURIES TO THE LOWER JAW

Jaw fractures usually result from direct force. A blow to one side of the jaw may fracture the other side. A fall on to the point of the chin can fracture both sides. A blow, or yawning, may dislocate the jaw.

Recognition
- Pain and sickness when moving the jaw. ◆ Distortion of the teeth and dribbling ◆ Swelling, tenderness, and bruising.
- A wound or bruising in mouth.

TREATMENT

YOUR AIMS ARE:
- To protect the airway.
- To arrange removal to hospital.

1 Help a casualty who is not seriously injured to sit up with her head well forward, to allow any blood, mucus, or saliva to drain away. Encourage the casualty to spit out any loose teeth.

IF she vomits, support her jaw and head, then gently clean out her mouth.

2 Give the casualty a soft pad to hold against her jaw and ask her to hold it firmly in place to support the jaw.

DO NOT bandage the pad in place.

3 Take or send the casualty to hospital, keeping her jaw supported.

INJURIES TO THE UPPER LIMB

The term "upper limb" is used to describe the shoulder girdle (the collar bone and shoulder) and the arm. Casualties with injuries to the upper limb can often walk or be transported to hospital seated.

FRACTURED COLLAR BONE

Collar bones form struts between shoulders and breastbone. It is rare for them to be broken by a direct blow. They are usually broken by indirect force, from impact at the shoulder or a fall on to an outstretched hand.

Recognition

◆ Pain and tenderness at the site of the injury, increased by movement.
◆ Possible attempts to relax muscles and relieve pain; the casualty may support the arm at the elbow, and incline the head to the injured side.

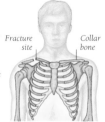

Fracture site

Collar bone

TREATMENT

YOUR AIMS ARE:

■ To immobilise the injured upper limb.
■ To arrange removal to hospital.

1 Sit the casualty down. Place the arm on her injured side across her chest, and ask her to support it at the elbow.

Rest fingertips against opposite shoulder

Head inclined to injured side

Support elbow

2 Support the arm in an elevation sling (*see page 123*).

3 Gently place soft padding, such as a small towel or folded clothing, between the injured arm and body to make the casualty more comfortable.

4 Secure the arm to the chest with a broad-fold bandage (*see page 121*) tied around the chest and over the sling.

Casualty should be able to straighten head once sling is applied

Elevation sling

Knot on uninjured side

Apply broad-fold bandage

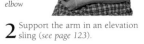

5 Take or send the casualty to hospital, keeping her seated.

DISLOCATED SHOULDER

A fall on to the shoulder or on to an outstretched arm, or a wrenching force, may cause the top of the arm bone to come out of the shoulder joint socket. Some people have repeated dislocations until a strengthening operation is carried out.

Recognition
- Severe pain, increased by movement.
- Reluctance to move because of the pain.
- Casualty may support the arm, and incline the head to the injured side.
- A flat, angular look to the shoulder.

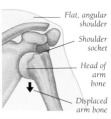

Flat, angular shoulder

Shoulder socket

Head of arm bone

Displaced arm bone

TREATMENT

YOUR AIMS ARE:
- To support the injured limb.
- To arrange removal to hospital.

1 Sit the casualty down. Gently place the affected arm across her chest at the angle that causes the least pain.

2 Place a triangular bandage between the affected limb and the chest, as for an arm sling (see page 123).

3 Insert soft padding between the arm and the chest (see page 121).

Pad between arm and body with folded fabric, triangular bandage, or cotton wool

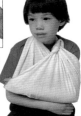

4 Finish tying the arm sling so that the arm and its padding are supported.

DO NOT attempt to replace the bone into its socket.
DO NOT allow food or drink, as an anaesthetic may be necessary.

5 Take or send the casualty to hospital, keeping her seated.

SHOULDER SPRAIN
A fall on to the shoulder may sprain ligaments that brace the collar bone at the shoulder. Some sprains, common in older people, affect the shoulder joint's capsule and tendons. Follow RICE treatment (see page 66).

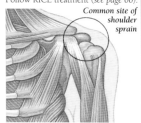

Common site of shoulder sprain

FRACTURED UPPER ARM

The long bone of the upper arm may be fractured across its shaft by a blow, but more commonly, especially in the elderly, the neck of the arm bone at the shoulder breaks, usually in a fall.

Because this type of fracture is a stable injury, a casualty may put up with the pain and walk around with an untreated fracture for some time without seeking medical advice.

Recognition
◆ Pain, increased by movement.
◆ Tenderness over the fracture site.
◆ Rapid swelling.
◆ Bruising, which may develop more slowly.

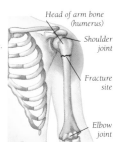

Head of arm bone (humerus)

Shoulder joint

Fracture site

Elbow joint

TREATMENT

YOUR AIMS ARE:
■ To immobilise the arm.
■ To arrange removal to hospital.

Ask casualty to support injured arm

Make casualty comfortable

1 Sit the casualty down. Gently place the injured arm across her chest in the position that is most comfortable. Ask her to support the arm, if possible.

2 Place the affected arm in an arm sling (*see page 123*), and place soft padding between the arm and the chest.

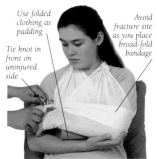

Use folded clothing as padding

Avoid fracture site as you place broad-fold bandage

Tie knot in front on uninjured side

3 Secure the limb to the chest by tying a broad-fold bandage (*see page 121*) around the chest and over the sling.

4 Take or send the casualty to hospital, keeping her seated.

INJURIES AROUND THE ELBOW

Elbow fractures are common, often resulting from a fall on to the hand. A fracture or dislocation of the forearm bones is characterised by a stiff elbow that cannot be fully straightened.

Children often fracture the upper arm bone above the elbow. This injury may cause broken bone ends to move and damage blood vessels and nerves, so monitoring the wrist pulse is vital.

Recognition
◆ Pain, increased by movement.
◆ Tenderness over the fracture site.
◆ Possible swelling and bruising.
◆ Fixed elbow if the head of the radius is fractured.

Arm bone (humerus)
Fracture site
Point of risk to artery
Radius
Ulna

TREATMENT

YOUR AIMS ARE:
■ To immobilise the arm without further injury to the joint.
■ To arrange removal to hospital.

FOR AN ELBOW THAT CAN BEND

Treat as for a fracture of the upper arm (*see page 70*). Check the affected wrist pulse every ten minutes.

IF the pulse is not present, gently straighten the elbow until the pulse returns and support it in that position.

FOR AN ELBOW THAT CANNOT BEND

DO NOT try to move injured limb.

1 Lay the casualty down. Use cushions or towels to pad around the elbow for comfort and support.

2 ☎ *DIAL 999 FOR AN AMBULANCE.* Check the injured wrist pulse every ten minutes until help arrives.

DO NOT attempt to bandage if medical help is on its way.

IF it is necessary to transport the casualty, put soft padding between the injured limb and body. Bandage the injured limb to the trunk, first at the wrist and hips, then above and below the elbow.

Casualty may be more comfortable lying down

Use towels and pillows as padding

INJURIES TO THE FOREARM AND WRIST

The forearm bones may be fractured by a heavy blow. As there is little fleshy covering, these fractures are often open, that is, with a wound.

The most common wrist fracture is a Colles' fracture (see right), usually suffered by older women who fall on to an outstretched hand. In a young adult, such a fall may break a wrist bone. The wrist joint is rarely dislocated, but often sprained, although it can be hard to distinguish between the two, especially if the scaphoid bone (see right) is hurt.

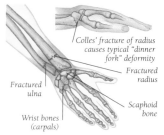

Colles' fracture of radius causes typical "dinner fork" deformity

Fractured radius

Fractured ulna

Scaphoid bone

Wrist bones (carpals)

TREATMENT

YOUR AIMS ARE:
- To immobilise the arm.
- To arrange removal to hospital.

1 Sit the casualty down. Gently steady and support the injured arm across his chest. If necessary, carefully treat any wound (see page 64).

Ask casualty to support injured arm

Place padding around injury

2 Place a triangular bandage between the chest and the injured arm, as for an arm sling (see page 123). Gently surround the forearm in soft padding.

3 Support the arm with its padding in an arm sling (see page 123).

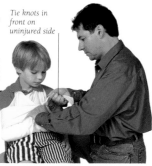

Tie knots in front on uninjured side

4 You may, if necessary, secure the limb to the chest, using a broad-fold bandage (see page 121). Tie the bandage over the sling, positioning it close to the elbow.

5 Take or send the casualty to hospital, keeping him seated.

INJURIES TO THE HAND AND FINGERS

Any one of the many small bones and movable joints in the hand may be injured by direct or indirect force.

Minor fractures are usually caused by direct force. Most commonly, an injury results from a misdirected punch and consists of a knuckle fracture between the little finger and the hand. Multiple fractures, affecting all the hand bones, are usually caused by crushing injuries, and may cause bleeding and swelling.

Any finger can be dislocated or sprained. Falls on to the hand are a common cause of a dislocated thumb.

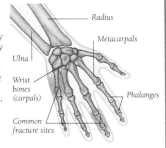

Radius

Metacarpals

Ulna

Wrist bones (carpals)

Phalanges

Common fracture sites

TREATMENT

YOUR AIMS ARE:
- To immobilise and elevate the hand.
- To arrange removal to hospital.

Pad hand with cotton wool or soft fabric

Support wrist

Ask casualty to support arm

1 Remove any rings before the hand begins to swell and keep the hand raised to reduce swelling. Protect the injured hand by wrapping it in folds of soft padding.

2 Gently support the affected arm in an elevation sling (*see page 124*).

3 You may, if necessary, secure the arm to the chest by tying a broad-fold bandage (*see page 121*) around the chest and over the sling.

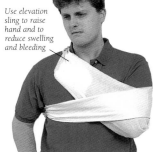

Use elevation sling to raise hand and to reduce swelling and bleeding

4 Take or send the casualty to hospital, keeping him seated.

FRACTURES OF THE RIBCAGE

Ribs may be fractured by direct force, from a blow or fall, or by indirect force from a crush injury. A fracture with a wound can impair breathing.

Flail chest injuries

Multiple rib injuries can cause the chest wall to move abnormally: going in when the casualty breathes in, and out when he breathes out. This "paradoxical breathing" causes severe respiratory difficulties.

Recognition

◆ Sharp pain at the fracture site.
◆ Pain on taking a deep breath.
◆ Shallow breathing.
◆ Paradoxical breathing.
◆ An open wound over the fracture, through which you might hear air being "sucked" into the chest cavity.
◆ Features of internal bleeding (see page 47) and shock (see page 32).

See also:
Chest Wounds, *page 45.*

TREATMENT

YOUR AIMS ARE:
■ To support the chest wall.
■ To arrange removal to hospital.

FOR A FRACTURED RIB

Support the limb on the injured side in an arm sling (see page 123). Take or send the casualty to hospital.

FOR OPEN OR MULTIPLE FRACTURES

1 Immediately cover and seal any wounds to the chest wall (see page 45).

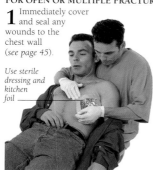

Use sterile dressing and kitchen foil

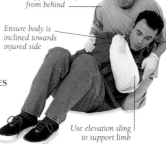

Support casualty from behind

Ensure body is inclined towards injured side

Use elevation sling to support limb

2 Put casualty in a comfortable position; this may be half-sitting, head, shoulders, and body turned to the injured side. Support limb on the injured side in a sling (see page 124).

☎ DIAL 999 FOR AN AMBULANCE.

IF he becomes unconscious, or has laboured breathing, put in the recovery position (see page 12), good side up.

SPINAL INJURY

This injury may affect the spinal cord, especially at neck level. If the cord is injured, there may be loss of power or sensation below the injury. Temporary damage can be caused if cord or nerve roots are pinched by displaced discs or bone; permanent injury results if the cord is partly or completely severed.

Dangers of spinal fracture

The spinal cord may be injured without damage to bones, but spinal fracture vastly increases this risk. Such fractures can be caused by direct or indirect force. The most vulnerable parts of the spine are the bones in the neck and lower back.

What causes spinal injury?

Suspect spinal injury when abnormal forces have been exerted on the back or neck, especially if the casualty has disturbed feeling or movement. If there was a violent forward bend, backward bend, or spinal twist, treat as a spinal fracture (*see overleaf*).

Recognition *When only the spinal bones are damaged, there may be:*
◆ Pain in the neck or back at the level of the injury; this may be masked by other painful injuries.
◆ A step, irregularity, or twist in the normal curve of the spine.
◆ Tenderness on feeling the spine.
When the cord is injured, there may be:
◆ Loss of control over limbs; movement may be weak or absent.
◆ Loss of sensation.
◆ Abnormal sensations, for example, burning or tingling. Limbs may feel "stiff", "heavy", or "clumsy".
◆ Breathing difficulties.

SOME CAUSES OF SPINAL INJURY
◆ Falling from a height.
◆ Falling awkwardly while doing gymnastics or trampolining.
◆ Diving into a shallow pool and hitting the bottom.
◆ Falling off a horse or motorbike.
◆ Being in a collapsed rugby scrum.
◆ Sudden deceleration in a vehicle.
◆ A heavy object falling on the back.
◆ Injury to the head or the face.

Check for spinal cord injury
Examine casualty carefully in the position found.

Ask helper to support head

Touch casualty without him knowing to test for loss of sensation

Ask him to move his limbs to test for loss of power

SPINAL INJURY: CONSCIOUS

YOUR AIMS ARE:
- To prevent further injury.
- To arrange urgent removal to hospital.

> **DO NOT** move the casualty from the position found, unless she is in danger or becomes unconscious (*see opposite*). If she must be moved, use a log-roll (*see opposite*).

1 Reassure the casualty, and tell her not to move.

Steady head and take care not to pull at neck

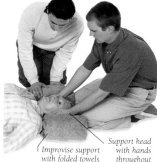

Improvise support with folded towels | *Support head with hands throughout*

2 Support head in the neutral position (*see page 79*) with your hands over her ears. Maintain support throughout.

IF you suspect neck injury, get a helper to roll up blankets or clothing on either side of neck and shoulders. ☎ *DIAL 999 FOR AN AMBULANCE.*

IF the ambulance's arrival is imminent, maintain support of the head and the neck with your hands until it arrives.

IF the ambulance is delayed and the neck is injured, apply a collar. Support head and neck firmly at all times.

MAKING A COLLAR

1 Fold a newspaper. Wrap it in a triangular bandage or scarf, or insert it into a pair of tights or a stocking.

2 Bend the wrapped newspaper over your thigh. Place the centre of the collar at the front of the neck, below the chin.

3 Gently pass the loose ends around the neck and tie at the front. Ensure that breathing is not impeded.

SPINAL INJURY: UNCONSCIOUS

YOUR AIMS ARE:
- To resuscitate casualty if necessary.
- To maintain an open airway.
- To prevent further damage to the spine or spinal cord.
- To arrange urgent removal to hospital.

Check breathing and pulse. Move casualty if resuscitation is required, even at risk of exacerbating injury.

BREATHING AND PULSE PRESENT

Place the casualty in a modified recovery position (*see overleaf*).
☎ *DIAL 999 FOR AN AMBULANCE.*

BREATHING AND PULSE ABSENT

1 ☎ *DIAL 999 FOR AN AMBULANCE.* Open and clear airway (*see page 11*). Gently tilt head so that head and neck stay in neutral position (*see overleaf*).

2 Recheck breathing and pulse. If not present, position casualty using the log-roll technique (*see below*).

3 Combine ventilations (*see pages 14–15*) with compressions (*see page 17*) until help arrives. If breathing and pulse return, place the casualty in a modified recovery position (*see overleaf*).

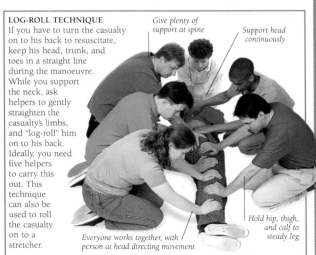

LOG-ROLL TECHNIQUE

If you have to turn the casualty on to his back to resuscitate, keep his head, trunk, and toes in a straight line during the manoeuvre. While you support the neck, ask helpers to gently straighten the casualty's limbs, and "log-roll" him on to his back. Ideally, you need five helpers to carry this out. This technique can also be used to roll the casualty on to a stretcher.

Give plenty of support at spine

Support head continuously

Hold hip, thigh, and calf to steady leg

Everyone works together, with person at head directing movement

THE RECOVERY POSITION IN SPINAL INJURY

If the casualty is unconscious with breathing and circulation present, put him in the recovery position (*see page 12*) to protect the airway. Ideally, with spinal injuries, modify the position to align the head and trunk at all times so that the spine is protected. You will need at least one helper to do this successfully; use more helpers if available. If alone with the casualty, the ABC of resuscitation (*see page 8*) must be followed, and the casualty must be turned to protect the airway, even if there is a risk of damaging the spine.

METHOD

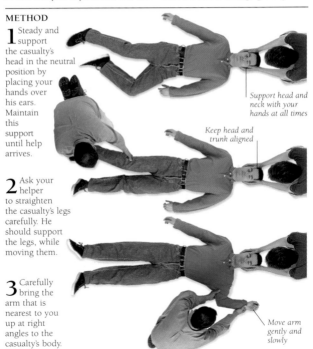

1 Steady and support the casualty's head in the neutral position by placing your hands over his ears. Maintain this support until help arrives.

Support head and neck with your hands at all times

Keep head and trunk aligned

2 Ask your helper to straighten the casualty's legs carefully. He should support the legs, while moving them.

3 Carefully bring the arm that is nearest to you up at right angles to the casualty's body.

Move arm gently and slowly

78

4 Your helper should grasp the casualty's opposite thigh, draw up the knee, and then bring the casualty's other arm across his chest. Your helper is now in the correct position to turn the casualty.

Bending leg will not harm spine

Helper simultaneously grasps thigh and shoulder

5 Ask your helper to pull casualty towards him until his body is on its side. Control the neutral position of the head and neck.

Maintain support at head

6 Ask your helper to adjust the top leg and, if necessary, to adjust the hand under the cheek so that the head remains tilted back. Your helper should help to support the casualty at the thigh and shoulder from either side, while you support the head and neck. If possible, stay like this until help arrives.

DO NOT pull on the neck.

Maintain support at head

Hip and knee should be at right angles

IF you have to send your helper to get aid, place rolled blankets, coats, or material on either side of casualty to keep him steady until help arrives.

IF the neck is injured, a collar may be applied for further support (*see page 76*). This is *not* a substitute for supporting the neck with the hands.

THE NEUTRAL HEAD POSITION
The least harmful position for a suspected spinal injury is a neutral one, with head, neck, and spine aligned. When moving the head, grip it firmly over the ears; move it slowly into position. Check that the nose is in line with the navel.

FRACTURED PELVIS

Pelvic injuries are usually caused by indirect force, such as in a car crash. The impact of a dashboard on a knee can force the thigh bone through the hip socket. The injury may be complicated by damage to internal tissues and organs, such as the bladder and urethra. Because of surrounding body tissue, internal bleeding may be severe, and shock often develops.

Recognition

◆ Inability to walk or even stand, although the legs appear uninjured.
◆ Pain and tenderness in the region of the hip, groin, or back, increased when the casualty moves.
◆ Blood at the urinary orifice, especially in a male casualty. Casualty may be unable to pass urine or find this painful.
◆ Signs of shock and internal bleeding.

See also:
Internal Bleeding, page 47.
Shock, page 32.

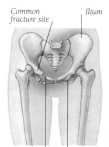

Common fracture site   *Ilium*

Pubis   *Ischium*

The pelvic girdle
Two hip bones formed by the fusions of the ischium, the ilium, and the pubis.

TREATMENT

YOUR AIM IS:
■ To arrange urgent removal to hospital.

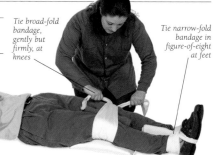

Tie broad-fold bandage, gently but firmly, at knees

Tie narrow-fold bandage in figure-of-eight at feet

Keep head low to minimise shock

1 Help the casualty to lie on his back either with his legs straight or, if it is more comfortable, help him to bend his knees slightly and support them.

2 Immobilise legs by bandaging together; pad between bony points.

3 ☎ *DIAL 999 FOR AN AMBULANCE.* Treat him for shock (*see page 32*).

DO NOT bandage the legs together if this causes intolerable pain.

INJURIES TO THE LOWER LIMB

Injuries to the lower limb, from the hip joint to the toes, include fractures, dislocations, sprains, and strains. It is important that casualties with lower limb injuries do not put weight on the injured leg.

INJURIES TO THE KNEE JOINT

This hinge joint is between thigh bone and shin bone. It can bend, straighten, and rotate. It is supported by muscles and ligaments, and protected by the kneecap. It can be injured by blows, twists, or strains.

Recognition
- A recent twist or blow to the knee.
- Pain in the joint.
- If the bent knee has "locked", acute pain on trying to straighten leg.
- Rapid swelling at the knee joint.

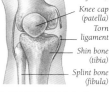

Thigh bone (femur)

Knee cap (patella)

Torn ligament

Shin bone (tibia)

Splint bone (fibula)

TREATMENT

YOUR AIMS ARE:
- To protect the knee in the most comfortable position.
- To arrange transport to hospital.

1 Help the casualty to lie down. Place padding, such as a blanket, under her injured knee to support it in the most comfortable position.

DO NOT attempt to straighten the knee forcibly. Displaced cartilage or internal bleeding may make the joint impossible to straighten safely.
DO NOT give the casualty anything to eat or drink; she may need an anaesthetic.
DO NOT allow the casualty to walk.

2 Wrap soft padding around the joint, and bandage it carefully in place.

3 Arrange for the casualty to be taken to hospital on a stretcher.

Keep your body clear of injury as you work

Use roller bandage to hold padding in place

Support casualty's knee with pillow, folded blanket, or coat

INJURIES TO THE HIP AND THIGH

It takes considerable force (such as in road accidents or falls from heights) to fracture the *shaft* of the thigh bone. This is a serious injury because, usually, a large volume of blood is lost into the tissues, which may cause shock.

Fractures of the *neck* of the thigh bone at the hip joint are common in the elderly, particularly in women, whose bones become more porous and brittle as they age. This can be a stable injury: the casualty may be able to walk around for some time before the fracture is discovered. The hip may also, more rarely, be dislocated.

Recognition
◆ Pain at the site of the injury.
◆ Inability to walk.
◆ Signs of shock.
◆ Shortening of the thigh, as powerful muscles pull broken bone ends together.
◆ Knee and foot are turned outwards.

See also:
Shock, page 32.

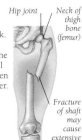

Hip joint — *Neck of thigh bone (femur)*

Fracture of shaft may cause extensive bleeding

TREATMENT

YOUR AIMS ARE:
■ To immobilise the lower limb.
■ To arrange urgent removal to hospital.

1 Lay the casualty down gently. Ask a helper to steady and support the injured limb.

3 ☎ *DIAL 999 FOR AN AMBULANCE.* If the ambulance is expected to arrive quickly, support the leg with your hands until it arrives.

Support injured limb while traction is applied at ankle

Pull ankle firmly and steadily away from knee in line of limb

2 Gently straighten the lower leg and apply traction (*see page 65*) at the ankle, if appropriate.

DO NOT give the casualty anything to eat or drink.

SNAKE BITES

The only poisonous snake native to mainland Britain is the adder, and its bite is rarely fatal. However, exotic snakes are kept as pets. A bite can be frightening. Reassure the casualty; it is vital for her to keep still and calm so the spread of venom is delayed. If you can, secure the snake in a container (take care, as its venom is active whether dead or alive). Or, note its appearance; this may help the correct anti-venom to be given. Notify police of the snake.

Recognition (*depending on species*)
◆ A pair of puncture marks.
◆ Severe pain at the site of the bite.
◆ Redness and swelling around bite.
◆ Nausea and vomiting.
◆ Laboured breathing.
◆ Disturbed vision.
◆ Increased salivation and sweating.

TREATMENT

YOUR AIMS ARE:
■ To reassure the casualty.
■ To prevent the spread of venom through the body.
■ To arrange urgent removal of the casualty to hospital.

1 Lay the casualty down. Tell her to keep calm and still.

☎ *DIAL 999 FOR AN AMBULANCE.*

2 Wash the wound well and pat dry with clean swabs.

Keep heart above level of wounded part to contain venom locally

DO NOT apply a tourniquet, slash the wound with a knife, or suck out the venom.

3 Lightly compress the limb above the wound with a roller bandage. Immobilise the injury (*see pages 64–65*).

IF she stops breathing, be ready to resuscitate (*see pages 8–22*) if needed.

Tie narrow-fold bandage in figure-of-eight around ankles and feet

Broad-fold bandage

Soft padding

DRESSINGS AND BANDAGES

11

Applying dressings and bandages is an important part of first aid. Wounds usually need a dressing, and most injuries benefit from the support of a bandage.

The materials needed for a first-aid kit, and how to use them, are shown in this chapter. The type of dressing or bandage and the technique for applying it, depends on the injury and materials available. Use sterile equipment if available, or improvise with clean, everyday articles.

Checking circulation

Limbs can swell after an injury, so after bandaging, it is vital to check circulation in a hand or foot immediately and then every ten minutes until help arrives. Press a nail until pale. If, on releasing pressure, colour does not return to the nail, or returns slowly, you should loosen the bandage.

DRESSINGS ARE USED TO:
♦ Help control bleeding. ♦ Cover a wound and protect it, thereby reducing the risk of infection.

BANDAGES ARE USED TO:
♦ Maintain direct pressure over a dressing to control bleeding. ♦ Hold dressings, compresses, and splints in place. ♦ Limit swelling. ♦ Support an injured limb or joint. ♦ Restrict movement.

FIRST-AID MATERIALS

The materials necessary for first-aid are usually kept in a first-aid kit or other suitable container. Kits should be kept at work, at sports and leisure facilities, in your home and car. The contents of a kit (*see overleaf*) for a workplace or leisure centre must conform to legal requirements; they should also be marked and readily accessible. The contents should form the basis of your kit at home, although you may wish to add to it.

Keep a first-aid kit in a dry atmosphere, and check and replenish it regularly, so that the items you need are always ready to use.

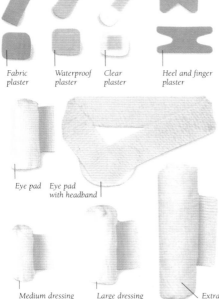

Fabric plaster   *Waterproof plaster*   *Clear plaster*   *Heel and finger plaster*

Eye pad   *Eye pad with headband*

Medium dressing   *Large dressing*   *Extra-large dressing*

DRESSINGS

Adhesive dressings or plasters
Use for minor wounds. The waterproof types are the best choice for wounds on the hands.

Sterile eye pads
Any injury to the eye needs the protection of a sterile covering.

Sterile dressings
These are easy to apply, so are ideal in an emergency. They come in a range of sizes, and are sealed in a protective wrapping.

First-aid Materials (CONTINUED)

BANDAGES

*Elasticated
roller bandage*

*Conforming
roller bandage*

*Crêpe conforming
roller bandage*

Roller bandages
Use these to give
support to joints,
secure dressings,
restrict movement,
maintain pressure
on a dressing, or
limit swelling.

*Crêpe
roller bandage*

*Open-weave
roller bandage*

*Self-adhesive
roller bandage*

*Folded cloth
triangular bandage*

*Folded paper
triangular bandage*

Triangular bandages
Made of cloth or strong
paper, these can be used
as bandages and slings.
If they are sterile and
individually wrapped,
they may be used as
dressings for large
wounds and burns.

Tubular grip for limbs

Finger gauze

Finger gauze applicator

Tubular bandages
Use these specially
shaped bandages on
joints and digits.

Basic materials for a first-aid kit

- Easily identifiable watertight box;
- 20 adhesive dressings (plasters) in assorted sizes;
- six medium sterile dressings;
- two large sterile dressings;

- two extra-large sterile dressings;
- two sterile eye pads;
- six triangular bandages;
- six safety pins;
- disposable gloves.

OTHER USEFUL ITEMS

Scissors

Safety pins

Clip

Tweezers

Adhesive tape
Use to fix
bandages in place.
Some people are
allergic to the
adhesive, so check
before applying.

Pins and clips
Secure bandages or
dressings with these.

Scissors and tweezers
Make sure scissors are
blunt-ended so that
they do not cause
injury.

Wound cleansing wipes
Clean skin
around small
wounds or your
hands with
these, if water
and soap are
not available.

Cotton wool
Never put on
wound; use as an
outer layer, or as
padding.

Blanket, torch, and whistle
Add these to outdoor
or camping first-aid kits.
The blanket can protect
a casualty from cold and
a whistle will help
rescuers locate you.

Disposable gloves
Wear gloves when
dressing wounds
or disposing of any
waste materials.

Tags
Use to label
casualties of
major accidents.

Gauze pads
Use as dressings,
for extra padding,
or as swabs.

Plastic face shield
This can protect you
when giving
artificial ventilation.

Notepad and pencil
Use to record a
casualty's details and
your observations.

Survival bags
These keep a
casualty warm
and dry.

Useful additions
◆ two crêpe roller bandages;
◆ scissors; ◆ tweezers;
◆ cotton wool; ◆ non-alcoholic
wound cleansing wipes;

◆ adhesive tape;
◆ notepad, pencil, and tags;
◆ plastic face shield;
◆ for outdoor activities: blanket,
survival bag, torch, and whistle.

STERILE DRESSINGS

These are dressing pads attached to a roller bandage. The pad is gauze or lint backed by cotton wool. They come in various sizes, sealed in wrappings. If a seal is broken, the dressing is no longer sterile.

METHOD

1 Remove the wrapping. Unwind the bandage's loose end; take care not to drop the roll or touch the dressing pad.

> **DO NOT** bandage so tightly that the circulation is impaired.

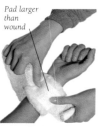

Pad larger than wound

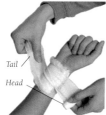

Tail

Head

Head

Tail

2 Unfold the dressing pad, holding the bandage on each side of the pad. Put the pad directly on to the wound.

3 Wind the short end, or *tail*, of the bandage once around the limb and dressing to secure the pad; leave it hanging.

4 Wind other end, or *head*, of the bandage around the limb to cover the whole pad, and leave the *tail* hanging free.

IF dressing slips, remove and apply a new one.

5 To secure bandage, tie the ends in a reef knot (*see page 122*), tied over the pad to exert pressure on the wound.

IF blood appears, do not remove dressing. Apply another dressing on top.

6 Check the bandage is not too tight (*see page 114*). Loosen if needed.

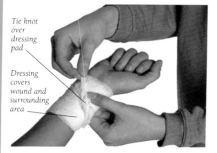

Tie knot over dressing pad

Dressing covers wound and surrounding area

ADHESIVE DRESSINGS

Used for small wounds, these consist of a gauze or cellulose pad on an adhesive backing and come in various sizes. Check casualty is not allergic to plasters. Food handlers use blue waterproof plasters.

METHOD

1 Dry the surrounding area. Remove the wrapping and hold the dressing, pad-side down, by its protective strips.

2 Peel back, but do not remove, the protective strips. Without touching the pad, place it on to the wound.

3 Carefully pull away the protective strips. Press ends and edges down.

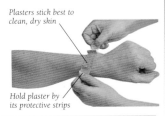

Plasters stick best to clean, dry skin

Hold plaster by its protective strips

COLD COMPRESSES

Cooling an injury, such as a bruise, reduces swelling and pain, but will not alter the severity of the injury. Use an ice pack or cold compress, or place injury under cold running water or in a basin of cold water. You can also use a pack of frozen vegetables wrapped in a cloth.

APPLYING A COLD PAD

Wring pad out lightly

1 Soak a flannel or towel in very cold water. Wring it out lightly; place firmly over injury and surrounding area.

2 Re-soak the pad in cold water every 3–5 minutes to keep it cold. Cool the injury for at least 20 minutes.

APPLYING AN ICE PACK

1 Partly fill a plastic bag with small ice cubes or crushed ice. Seal and wrap in a bandage or a cloth.

Press firmly

2 Hold the ice pack firmly in place over the injury.

3 Cool the injury for 10–15 minutes only, replacing the ice as necessary.

APPLYING A ROLLER BANDAGE

Follow these general rules when you are applying a roller bandage.

◆ When the bandage is partly unrolled, the roll is called the "head", and the unrolled part, the "tail". Keep the *head* of the bandage uppermost when bandaging.

◆ Stand in front at the injured side.
◆ While working, support injury in position it will stay in after bandaging.
◆ Check the bandage is not too tight, especially conforming and crêpe ones; these mould to the shape of the limb, and can tighten if the limb swells.

METHOD

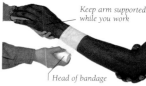

Keep arm supported while you work

Head of bandage

1 Place the *tail* of the bandage below the injury and, working from the inside of the limb outwards, make two straight turns with the *head* of the bandage to anchor it in place.

Make straight turn to finish

3 Finish off with one straight turn, and secure the end (*see opposite*).

IF the bandage is too short, apply another one in the same way to extend it.

Keep head of bandage uppermost

2 Make a series of spiralling turns, winding from the inside to the outside of the limb and working up the limb. Make sure that each turn covers between a half and two-thirds of the previous layer of bandaging.

Press nail to check circulation

4 Check that the bandage is not too tight: press a nail; if colour returns slowly then the bandage is too tight.

IF the bandage is too tight, partially undo it, and re-apply it more loosely.

TRIANGULAR BANDAGES

Sold in sterile packs, these can also be made by cutting or folding a square metre of fabric (such as linen) diagonally in half. They can be used:

♦ folded into broad-fold bandages (*see below, right*) to immobilise and support limbs and secure splints and bulky dressings;

♦ folded into narrow-fold bandages (*see below*), to immobilise feet and ankles, and hold dressings in place;

♦ straight from a pack, folded to form a sterile improvised dressing;

♦ open, as slings, to support an injured limb, or to hold a hand, foot, or scalp dressing in position.

Open triangular bandage

— Point

| End | Base | End |

STORING A TRIANGULAR BANDAGE

Store the bandages in their packs, or in the way shown below so that, in an emergency, they are ready-folded for use or can be shaken open.

1 Start with a narrow-fold bandage (*see right*). Bring the two ends of the bandage into the centre.

2 Keep folding the ends into the centre until a handy size is reached. Keep the bandage in a dry place.

MAKING A BROAD-FOLD BANDAGE

| End | Point | Base |

1 Open out a triangular bandage and lay it flat on a clean surface. Fold it horizontally so that the *point* touches the centre of the *base*.

2 Fold the triangular bandage in half again in the same direction. This completes the broad-fold bandage.

MAKING A NARROW-FOLD BANDAGE

1 Fold a triangular bandage to make a broad-fold bandage (*see above*).

2 Fold the bandage horizontally in half again to make a thick, but long and narrow, bandage.

REEF KNOTS

When securing a bandage, use a reef knot. It lies flat so is comfortable for the casualty; it is secure and will not slip, but is easy to untie. Avoid tying the knot near the injury itself as this may cause discomfort.

TYING A REEF KNOT

1 Pass the left end (*dark*) over and under right.

3 Pass right end (*dark*) over and under left.

UNTYING A KNOT

1 Pull end and piece of bandage apart.

2 Bring both ends up again.

4 Pull ends firmly to tighten; tuck in ends.

2 Hold knot; pull the end through and out.

HAND AND FOOT COVER BANDAGE

An open triangular bandage on a hand will not exert enough pressure to control bleeding, but is useful for securing a dressing. This method for bandaging a hand can also be used on a foot; tie ends around the ankle.

METHOD

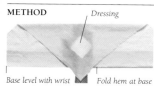

Dressing

Base level with wrist *Fold hem at base*

1 Lay the bandage flat. Place casualty's hand on it, fingers towards *point*. Dress the wound. Fold the *point* of the bandage over the hand, to the forearm.

Reef knot

2 Pass *ends* around wrist in opposite directions. Tie a reef knot over the *point*; pull *point* gently to tighten the bandage. Fold *point* over knot; tuck in.

SLINGS

Slings are used to support the arm of a casualty who is sitting or is able to walk. There are two types of sling:

◆ **arm sling** supports arm with the forearm horizontal or slightly raised; used for an injured upper arm, wrist, or forearm, or a simple rib fracture;

◆ **elevation sling** supports the upper limb with the hand in a well-raised position. This is used for some fractures, to help control bleeding from wounds in the forearm, to reduce swelling in burn injuries, and for complicated rib fractures.

APPLYING AN ARM SLING

1 Support injured arm so hand is above uninjured elbow. Pass one *end* of bandage through at injured elbow and pull to the opposite shoulder. Spread out bandage so *base* is level with little finger nail.

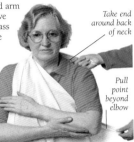

Take end around back of neck

Pull point beyond elbow

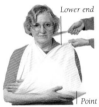

Lower end

Point

2 Bring lower *end* up over arm to meet other *end* at shoulder.

3 Tie a reef knot (*see page 122*) at hollow over her collar bone on the injured side. Tuck both *ends* of the bandage under the knot to pad it.

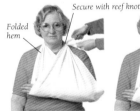

Folded hem

Secure with reef knot

4 Fold the *point* forward at her elbow. Tuck any loose bandage under; secure the *point* to the front of the bandage with a safety pin.

Pin at front of elbow

IF you do not have a pin, twist the *point* until the sling fits her elbow snugly; tuck it into sling at the back of her arm.

5 Check bandages every 10 minutes (*see page 114*). If too tight, undo sling and loosen bandages.

123

APPLYING AN ELEVATION SLING

Injured side

Point well beyond elbow of injured side

Base

Leave thumb showing

Support arm as you work

1 Ask the casualty to support the injured arm across his chest, with his fingertips touching the opposite shoulder.

2 Drape one *end* of a triangular bandage over his shoulder on the uninjured side, with the *point* on his injured side.

3 Ask the casualty to release his arm. Tuck the *base* of the bandage under his hand and arm and behind his elbow.

Bring ends up to shoulder

4 Bring the lower *end* up diagonally across his back to meet the other *end* at his shoulder.

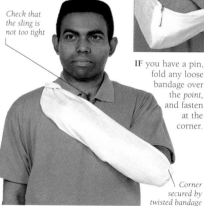

Check that the sling is not too tight

IF you have a pin, fold any loose bandage over the *point*, and fasten at the corner.

Corner secured by twisted bandage

5 Tie *ends* in reef knot (*see page 122*) at the hollow above collar bone. Tuck ends under knot.

6 Twist the *point* until bandage fits snugly at elbow. Tuck *point* into sling at elbow to secure.

7 Check sling is not too tight around fingers (*see page 114*). If it is, loosen any bandages.

INDEX

THE VOLUNTARY AID SOCIETIES

ST. JOHN AMBULANCE

St. John Ambulance is a charity providing:
◆ First Aid training and medical support services
◆ Caring services in support of community needs
◆ Personal and social development for young people.

Details of First Aid courses or volunteering can be obtained from your local St. John Ambulance office, listed in the telephone directory.

ST. ANDREW'S AMBULANCE ASSOCIATION

St. Andrew's Ambulance Association was founded in 1882, incorporated by Royal Charter in 1899, and today remains committed to its original mission of caring for Humanity.

The Association runs training courses in First Aid and allied subjects and provides voluntary First Aid cover at thousands of events throughout Scotland annually.

BRITISH RED CROSS

The British Red Cross cares for people in crisis at home and abroad. It gives vital impartial support during both major emergencies and personal crises, and provides comprehensive training in First Aid and caring skills.

The red cross emblem is a symbol of protection during armed conflict and its use is restricted by law.

OBSERVATION CHART

Fill in charts when treating casualty.
♦ On the first chart, put the score in the column after each check.

♦ On the second chart, tick the appropriate pulse or breathing rate.
♦ Send the form with the casualty.

DATE .... CASUALTY'S NAME							
LEVEL OF RESPONSE (Glasgow coma scale)							
Time of observation (10-minute intervals)		10	20	30	40	50	60
Eyes Observe for reaction while testing other responses.	Open spontaneously **4** Open to speech **3** Open to painful stimulus **2** No response **1**						
Speech When testing responses, speak clearly and directly, close to casualty's ear.	Responds sensibly to questions **5** Seems confused **4** Uses inappropriate words **3** Incomprehensible sounds **2** No response **1**						
Movement Apply painful stimulus: pinch ear lobe or skin on back of hand.	Obeys commands **6** Points to pain **5** Withdraws from painful stimulus **4** Bends in response to pain **3** Stretches in response to pain **2** No response **1**						
TOTAL SCORE							

PULSE AND BREATHING CHECK (*tick the appropriate box*)							
Time of observation (10-minute intervals)		10	20	30	40	50	60
Pulse (beats per minute) Take pulse at wrist or at neck on adult (*page 16*); at inner arm on baby (*page 21*). Note rate, and whether beats are weak (**w**) or strong (**s**), regular (**reg**) or irregular (**irreg**).	Over 110						
	101-110						
	91-100						
	81-90						
	71-80						
	61-70						
	Below 61						
Breathing (breaths per minute) Note rate, and whether breathing is quiet (**q**) or noisy (**n**), easy (**e**) or difficult (**diff**).	Over 40						
	31-40						
	21-30						
	11-20						
	below 11						

4 Take any steps possible to treat the casualty for shock; insulate him from the cold, but do not raise his legs.

IF the ambulance is delayed, immobilise the limb by securing or splinting it to the uninjured limb.
* Gently bring the casualty's sound limb alongside the injured one.
* Maintaining traction at the ankle, slide two bandages under the knees. Ease them above and below the fracture by sliding them back or forth. Position more bandages under knees and ankles.
* Insert padding between the thighs, knees, and ankles.

* Tie the bandages around his ankles and knees. Then tie the bandages above and below the fracture site.
* Release traction only when all bandaging knots are tied.

Tie feet together with narrow-fold figure-of-eight

Tuck ends under knot

Place soft padding between legs

Fracture site

Use broad-fold bandages around legs

TRANSPORTING A CASUALTY OVER DISTANCE

Log-roll casualty on to carrying canvas or blanket after bandaging

Splint from armpit to foot

1 2 5 6 4 7 3

Fracture site

If you move a casualty on a stretcher you will need a sturdy leg support. If trained, use a purpose-made malleable splint. Or place a leg splint, such as a post, from armpit to foot, against the injured side. Pad between legs and between splint and body. Secure splint with broad-fold bandages at chest (1), pelvis (2), ankles (3), knees (4), either side of fracture (5 and 6) and an extra point (7). *Do not* cover fracture. To move, use the log-roll technique (*see page 77*). Raise feet to reduce swelling and shock.

INJURIES TO THE LOWER LEG

The shin bone of the lower leg is usually only broken by a heavy blow (for example, from a moving vehicle). The thinner splint bone can be broken by the type of twisting injury that sprains the ankle. If the shin bone remains intact, the casualty may be able to walk, and be unaware of a fracture.

Recognition
+ Localised pain.
+ A recent blow or wrench of the foot.
+ An open wound.
+ Inability to walk.

Swelling and bruising

"Bumper bar" fracture

Shin bone (tibia)

Splint bone (fibula)

TREATMENT

YOUR AIMS ARE:
■ To immobilise the leg.
■ To arrange urgent removal to hospital.

1 Help the casualty to lie down. Steady and support the injured leg. If necessary, gently treat any wound (*see page 64*).

Support leg at knee and ankle

2 Straighten the leg using traction (*see page 65*); pull in the line of the shin.

TRANSPORTING THE CASUALTY
If you transport the casualty on a stretcher, pad either side of the legs, from the thigh to the foot. Place broad-fold bandages at the thigh and knee, and above and below fracture.

---

3 ☎ DIAL 999 FOR AN AMBULANCE. Support the leg with your hands until the ambulance arrives.

IF the ambulance is delayed, splint the injured limb to the sound one.
+ Bring sound limb to the injured one.

Pad with towels or clothing   *Fracture site*

Use broad-fold bandages

+ Gently slide two bandages under the knees and two under the ankles.
+ Pad between knees, ankles and calves.
+ Secure two of the bandages at the knees and ankles.
+ Secure remaining two bandages above and below the fracture site.

IF the ankle is broken, bandage above it and around the toes, rather than in a figure-of-eight.

BURNS AND SCALDS

7

Burns result from dry heat, extreme cold, corrosives, friction, or radiation, including the sun's rays; scalds result from wet heat from hot liquids and vapours.

Burns and scalds may be associated with conditions that pose a greater threat to life or there may be other injuries caused, for example, by a jump from a burning building. Once the burns are treated, the casualty should be thoroughly examined.

Dealing with a burns incident
The approach to an accident resulting in burns is frequently complicated by the presence of fire, an explosion, electricity, smoke, toxic fumes, or other dangerous hazards. Serious burns can be very distressing, and both you and the casualty may be upset by the smell of singed hair and burned flesh.

Check your own safety and the casualty's airway, then assess the extent and depth of the burn. The extent is calculated as a percentage of the total body surface. The depth describes the type of burn: a superficial burn causes redness, swelling, and tenderness; a partial-thickness burn causes blisters, and a full thickness burn causes damage to nerves and tissues.

FIRST-AID PRIORITIES
◆ Establish your safety before treating casualty.

◆ Check the airway.

◆ Cool the burn to limit tissue damage, swelling, shock, and pain.

◆ Cover the injury to protect from infection.

◆ Check other injuries.

◆ Assess the burns, unless very minor, and get medical aid.

SEVERE BURNS AND SCALDS

Take great care when treating deep or extensive burns or ones that extend over a large area. The longer burning continues, the more severe the injury. Also, if the casualty has been in a fire, it should be assumed that smoke or hot air has also affected the respiratory system.

The two essential priorities are to rapidly cool the burn, and to check breathing. Follow the ABC of resuscitation (see pages 8–22). A casualty with a severe burn or scald will probably be affected by shock and may require first aid.

See also:
Burns to the Airway, page 88.
Resuscitation, pages 8–22.
Shock, page 32.

TREATMENT

YOUR AIMS ARE:
- To stop the burning and relieve pain.
- To maintain an open airway.
- To treat associated injuries.
- To minimise the risk of infection.
- To arrange removal to hospital.
- To gather relevant information for the emergency services.

1 Lay the casualty down. Protect the burned area from contact with the ground, if possible.

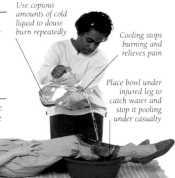

Use copious amounts of cold liquid to douse burn repeatedly

Cooling stops burning and relieves pain

Place bowl under injured leg to catch water and stop it pooling under casualty

2 Douse burn with cold liquid for at least 10 minutes or use a cooling gel. Don't delay removal to hospital.

3 While cooling the burn, watch for signs of difficulty in breathing; be ready to resuscitate (see pages 8–22).

☎ *DIAL 999 FOR AN AMBULANCE.*

DO NOT overcool the casualty; this could lower body temperature to a dangerous level (*hypothermia*) if the burns cover a large part of the body.
DO NOT remove anything sticking to the burn; you may cause further damage and introduce infection.

Cut away clothing around site of burn

Use blunt-tipped scissors

DO NOT touch or otherwise interfere with the injured area.
DO NOT burst any blisters.
DO NOT apply lotions, ointment, fat, or adhesive tape to the injury.

Hold clean pad by edges to avoid infection

Wear plastic gloves to reduce risk of infection

4 Gently remove any rings, watches, belts, shoes, or smouldering clothing from the injured area, before it begins to swell. Carefully remove burned clothing, unless it is sticking to the burn.

5 Cover injury with a sterile dressing or suitable material (*see box, below*) to protect it from germs and infection.

IF there is a facial burn, do not cover it. Cool a facial injury with water to relieve the pain until help arrives.

6 *Record* details of injuries, circumstances, and any hazards.

7 Reassure casualty; treat for shock. Record breathing and pulse rates; be ready to resuscitate, if necessary (*see pages 8–22*).

DRESSING A BURN

Burns and scalds must be protected from infection, but the dressing does not need to be secured unless on an awkward body part. Use a sterile dressing or improvise with clean, non-fluffy material, such as: a bit of clean sheet or pillowcase; plastic kitchen film – discard the first two turns of the roll; a folded triangular bandage; a clean plastic bag for a hand or foot – secured with a bandage or tape over the plastic, not the skin.

Clean bag protects burn

SPECIAL TYPES OF BURN

Many burns are caused not by contact with a naked flame, but by scorching air or heat produced within body tissues by, for example, electricity. The damage caused is the same as for thermal burns, and first aid follows the same principles.

If an accident involves high-voltage electricity or harmful chemicals, remember your own safety first. Do not endanger yourself or others by treating a casualty in hazardous circumstances, however urgent the casualty's needs appear.

BURNS TO THE AIRWAY

Burns to the face and in the mouth or throat are dangerous, as air passages become inflamed and swollen. Usually there is evidence of burning, but suspect airway burns if the injury has been sustained in a small space where hot air or gases may have been inhaled.

There is no specific first-aid treatment for an extreme case; the swelling will rapidly block the airway, and there is a serious risk of suffocation. Immediate and specialised medical aid is needed.

Recognition
◆ Soot around the nose or mouth.
◆ Singeing of the nasal hairs.
◆ Redness, swelling, or actual burning of the tongue.
◆ Damaged skin around the mouth.
◆ Hoarseness of the voice.
◆ Breathing difficulties.

See also:
Shock, *page 32.*

TREATMENT

YOUR AIMS ARE:
■ To get medical aid immediately.
■ To maintain an open airway.

1 ☎ *DIAL 999 FOR AN AMBULANCE.* Tell the control officer that you suspect burns to the airway.

2 Take any steps possible to improve the air supply; for example, loosen clothing around his neck. Give oxygen, if you are trained to do so.

IF the casualty becomes unconscious, open airway, check breathing; be ready to resuscitate (*see pages 8–22*). Place in recovery position (*see page 12*).

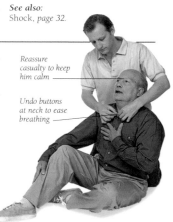

Reassure casualty to keep him calm

Undo buttons at neck to ease breathing

ELECTRICAL BURNS

These occur when electricity passes through the body. Visible damage is at the current's entry and exit points, but there may also be internal damage. The positioning of wounds indicates the likely extent of hidden injury and the degree of shock that may ensue.

Dangers of electrical burns

Burns may be caused by lightning or a low or high-voltage current. Electric shocks can cause cardiac arrest. If the casualty is unconscious, once you are sure the area is safe, check the ABC of resuscitation (see pages 8–22).

Recognition

◆ Unconsciousness.
◆ Full-thickness burns, with swelling, scorching, and charring, at both the point of entry and exit.
◆ Signs of shock.
◆ A brown, coppery residue on the skin, if the casualty has been a victim of "arcing" high-voltage electricity. (Do not mistake this for injury.)

See also:

Cardiac Arrest, *page 38.*
Severe Burns and Scalds, *page 86.*
Shock, *page 32.*

TREATMENT

YOUR AIMS ARE:
■ To treat the burns and shock.
■ To arrange removal of the casualty to hospital.

1 Make sure that contact with the electrical source is broken.

IF the casualty is unconscious, open the airway, check breathing; be ready to resuscitate (see pages 8–22).

2 Cool the burn with plenty of cold water (see page 86), and cut away any burned clothing if necessary.

3 Put a sterile dressing, a clean, folded triangular bandage, or other clean, non-fluffy material over the burn to protect against any airborne infection.

☎ *DIAL 999 FOR AN AMBULANCE.*

4 Reassure the casualty and treat for shock (see page 32).

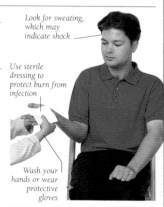

Look for sweating, which may indicate shock

Use sterile dressing to protect burn from infection

Wash your hands or wear protective gloves

DO NOT approach a victim of high-voltage electricity until you are officially informed that the current has been switched off and isolated.

CHEMICAL BURNS

Some chemicals irritate, harm, or are absorbed through skin; damage can be fatal. Unlike thermal burns, signs develop slowly, but first aid is the same.

Chemical burns can occur at home, especially from paint stripper, oven cleaner and dishwasher products. These burns are serious and may need urgent hospital treatment. Try to note the substance's name. Ensure your safety: some chemicals have deadly fumes.

Recognition
- Evidence of chemicals in the vicinity.
- Intense, stinging pain.
- Later, discolouration, blistering, peeling, and swelling of affected area.

See also:
Assess the
Situation,
page 5.

TREATMENT

YOUR AIMS ARE:
- To disperse the harmful chemical.
- To arrange transport to hospital.
- To make the area safe and inform the relevant authority.

Take care not to contaminate yourself: use protective gloves

1 First make sure that the area is safe. Ventilate the area and, if possible, seal the chemical container. Remove the casualty from the area if necessary.

Direct hose away from yourself to avoid splashes

Ask casualty if she can identify chemical

2 Flood affected area with water for at least 20 minutes to disperse the chemical and stop burning.

> **NEVER** attempt to neutralise acid or alkali burns unless trained to do so.
> **DO NOT** delay starting treatment by searching for an antidote.

3 Gently remove any contaminated clothing while flooding the injury.

4 Take or send casualty to hospital; watch airway and breathing. Pass on any details about the chemical.

IF in the workplace, notify the local Safety Officer or emergency services.

CHEMICAL BURNS TO THE EYE

Chemical splashes in the eye can cause serious injury if not treated quickly. The eye's surface can be damaged, causing scarring or blindness. When irrigating the eye, do not let contaminated water splash you or the casualty. Wear protective gloves if available.

Recognition
◆ Intense pain in the eye.
◆ Inability to open the injured eye.
◆ Redness and swelling around the eye.
◆ Copious watering of the eye.
◆ Evidence of chemical substances or containers in the immediate area.

TREATMENT

YOUR AIMS ARE:
■ To disperse the harmful chemical.
■ To arrange removal to hospital.

> **DO NOT** allow the casualty to touch the injured eye or forcibly remove contact lens.

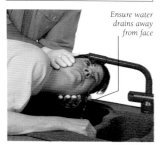

Ensure water drains away from face

2 Ask the casualty to hold a sterile eye pad or a pad of clean, non-fluffy material over the injured eye.

Put bandage over eye pad

IF some time elapses before the casualty receives medical attention, bandage the pad loosely in position.

3 Take or send the casualty to hospital. Identify the chemical, if possible.

1 Hold the eye under gently running cold water for at least ten minutes. Irrigate both sides of the eyelid well; or use a glass or eye irrigator.

IF the eye is shut in a spasm of pain, gently but firmly pull the eyelids open. Be careful that contaminated water does not splash the uninjured eye.

> **CS GAS**
> This spray, which is used to incapacitate, irritates the airway and eyes, but usually wears off after 15 minutes. It may trigger asthma (*see page 30*). Face the casualty to the wind; discourage rubbing of the eyes or face. Do not rinse eyes unless symptoms persist. If the casualty receives a big dose at close range, get her to hospital.

MINOR BURNS AND SCALDS

Small, superficial burns are often caused by domestic accidents or sunburn. Most are easily treated and will heal naturally. If you are in any doubt as to the severity of the injury, seek medical advice.

TREATMENT

YOUR AIMS ARE:
- To stop the burning.
- To relieve pain and swelling.
- To minimise the risk of infection.

Cool with plenty of water

1 Flood with cold water for at least ten minutes to relieve burning and pain. If water is not available, use any cold, harmless liquid, such as milk.

2 Gently remove jewellery, watches, belts, or constricting clothing from the injury before it begins to swell.

DO NOT break blisters or otherwise interfere with the injured area.
DO NOT apply adhesive dressings or tape to the skin; the burn may be more extensive than it first appears.
DO NOT apply lotions, ointments, or fats; they can further damage the tissues and increase risk of infection.

3 Cover the area with a sterile dressing, or any clean, non-fluffy material, and bandage loosely in place. A plastic bag or some kitchen film (*see page 87*) makes a good temporary covering.

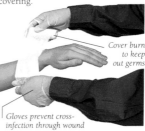

Cover burn to keep out germs

Gloves prevent cross-infection through wound

BLISTERS

These thin "bubbles" form on skin damaged by heat or friction. They are caused by tissue fluid leaking into the burned area below the skin's surface. During healing, new skin forms at the blister's base; the serum is re-absorbed and the outer layer of skin eventually peels off.

Never break a blister as you may cause infection. Blisters usually need no treatment. However, if it breaks, or may be damaged, cover the area with a dry, non-adhesive dressing that extends beyond the blister's edge until the blister subsides.

EFFECTS OF HEAT AND COLD

8

The human body is designed to work best at, or close to, a temperature of 37°C (98.6°F). To maintain this temperature, the body possesses mechanisms that generate and conserve heat when the environment is cold and, conversely, that lose heat when it is hot. These mechanisms are controlled by a special centre, or "thermostat" in the brain. In addition, humans control their environment to some degree through clothing, heating, and air-conditioning, making it easier for the body to perform well in a wide range of temperatures. In spite of all this, excessive heat or cold can still cause serious or even fatal injury.

The dangers of extreme temperatures

The harmful effects of extreme heat or cold can be localised, as is the case with frostbite and sunburn, or generalised, as with hypothermia, heat exhaustion, and heatstroke. The generalised effects of extremes of temperature tend to occur more often in the very young and in the very old, whose temperature-regulation systems may, respectively, be under-developed or impaired.

CONTENTS

THE FIRST AIDER SHOULD

◆ Remove, or protect, the casualty from excessively hot or cold surroundings.

◆ Restore normal body temperature: if the condition has been rapid in onset (for example, heat exhaustion), reverse it rapidly; if it has developed slowly (for example, hypothermia of slow onset affecting an elderly person), the body temperature should be gradually restored to normal.

◆ Get medical attention.

EFFECTS OF EXTREME COLD

The body reacts to cold by shutting down blood vessels in the skin to stop "core heat" escaping. When deprived of warm blood, extremities such as fingers or toes may freeze in severe conditions, causing frostbite. If the body's core temperature becomes dangerously low, bodily functions slow down (*hypothermia*) and may cease altogether.

FROSTBITE

This usually occurs in freezing and often dry and windy conditions. Those who cannot move are especially at risk. The tissues of the extremities freeze, in severe cases leading to permanent loss of sensation and, eventually, gangrene. Frostbite is often accompanied by hypothermia (*see pages 95–96*).

Recognition
◆ At first, "pins-and-needles".
◆ Paleness, followed by numbness.
◆ A hardening and stiffening of the skin.
◆ A colour change to the affected skin: first white; then mottled and blue; and eventually black; on recovery skin is red, hot, painful, and blistered.

TREATMENT

YOUR AIMS ARE:
■ To warm the affected area slowly, to prevent further tissue damage.
■ To obtain medical aid if necessary.

1 Very gently remove gloves, rings, and any other constrictions, such as boots. Warm the affected part with your hands, in your lap, or in the casualty's armpit. Avoid rubbing because it can damage skin and tissues.

Allow casualty to warm affected part

DO NOT put affected part by direct heat, or thaw it if there is danger of it refreezing.

2 Move casualty into warmth before thawing the affected part; carry her if possible when the feet are affected.

3 Place affected part in warm water. Dry carefully; apply a light dressing of fluffed-up, dry gauze bandage.

4 Raise and support the limb to reduce swelling. An adult may take two paracetamol tablets for intense pain. Get her to hospital, if necessary.

IMMERSION (TRENCH) FOOT
Occurs in near-freezing conditions; aggravated by tight shoes, wet socks, and immobility. Feet are white, cold, numb; then red, hot, and painful on rewarming. Treat as for frostbite.

Hypothermia

This develops when body temperature falls below 35°C (95°F). The effects vary with the speed of onset, and the level to which the temperature falls. It may develop over a few days in poorly heated houses. Infants and the elderly are especially at risk. It is also caused by prolonged exposure to cold outside.

See also:
Cardiac Arrest, *page 38*. Drowning, *page 28*.

Recognition
As hypothermia develops, there may be:
♦ Shivering, and cold, pale, dry skin.
♦ Apathy, disorientation, or irrational or belligerent behaviour.
♦ Lethargy or failing consciousness.
♦ Slow and shallow breathing.
♦ A slow and weakening pulse.
♦ In extreme cases, cardiac arrest.
See below for casualty indoors and overleaf for casualty outdoors.

TREATMENT

YOUR AIMS ARE:
■ To prevent the casualty losing more body heat.
■ To rewarm the casualty.
■ To obtain medical aid.

CASUALTY INDOORS

1 For a casualty brought in from outside, quickly replace any wet clothing with warm, dry garments.

2 The casualty can have a bath if fit, young, and can get in unaided. The water should be warm (40°C / 104°F).

Cover head for extra warmth
Stay until colour and warmth return to skin

3 Put the casualty to bed. Cover her well. Give her warm drinks, soup, or high-energy food like chocolate.

DO NOT place heat sources, such as hot-water bottles or fires, next to the casualty.
DO NOT give the casualty alcohol.

4 Call a doctor if you have any doubts about the casualty's condition.

IF the casualty becomes unconscious, open the airway, check breathing, and be ready to resuscitate (*see pages 8–22*).
☎ **DIAL 999 FOR AN AMBULANCE.**
Resuscitate, if needed, until help arrives.

HYPOTHERMIA IN INFANTS
A baby is especially vulnerable to cold. A baby with hypothermia may look well, but be cold, limp, quiet, and not feed. Slowly rewarm with blankets and heating. Call a doctor.

HYPOTHERMIA IN THE ELDERLY
As the body ages, it is less able to cope with temperature changes. Hypothermia indoors may develop slowly. Rewarm slowly, and avoid hot baths. Always call a doctor.

HYPOTHERMIA (CONTINUED)
CASUALTY OUTDOORS

DO NOT use a hot-water bottle or an electric blanket to try and warm the casualty.
DO NOT give the casualty alcohol.

Make sure casualty has enough clothing, but do not give him yours

1 Insulate the casualty with extra clothes or blankets. Cover his head.

2 Take or carry the casualty to a sheltered place as soon as possible.

3 Protect the casualty from the ground and the elements. Put him in a dry sleeping bag, cover him with blankets or newspapers, or enclose him in a plastic or foil survival bag.

Shelter and warm him with your body

PREVENTING HYPOTHERMIA OUTDOORS
Expeditions should be planned and supervised. Anyone with even minor illness should not take part; take anyone unwell or injured during the trip to safety at once.

Be equipped for an emergency
Take a spare sweater, socks, a dry, aired sleeping bag, survival bag, and high-energy food and drink; not alcohol. Layers of clothes are better than one warm garment. The outer layer should be wind- and water-proof, and able to be undone at neck and wrists. Coats and boots are heavy if wet; if you fall into water, lie still and remove them, as the weight may drag you down.

Lay casualty on thick layer of dry insulating material, such as pine branches, heather, or bracken

Protect him from wind and rain with survival bag

4 Send for help; in an ideal situation, two people should go. However, it is important that you do not leave the casualty alone; someone must remain with him at all times.

5 Give a conscious casualty warm drinks, if available.

6 When help arrives, evacuate the casualty to hospital by stretcher.

IF the casualty becomes unconscious, open the airway, check breathing, and be ready to resuscitate (*see pages 8–22*). If necessary, continue resuscitation until medical help arrives.

EFFECTS OF EXTREME HEAT

When atmospheric temperature is the same as body temperature, the body cannot lose heat by radiation or evaporation. If the atmosphere is also humid, sweat will not evaporate from the body. In these conditions, particularly during exercise when the body generates more heat, heat exhaustion or heatstroke can occur.

RECREATIONAL DRUG USE
A common cause of raised body temperature results from certain drugs, like Ecstasy. Profuse sweating from prolonged activity leads to dehydration and heat exhaustion. This, and the drug's effect on the brain, can cause heatstroke.

HEAT EXHAUSTION

This condition usually develops gradually and is caused by loss of salt and water from the body through excessive sweating. It usually happens to people who are unaccustomed to a hot, humid environment. Those who are unwell, especially with illnesses that cause vomiting and diarrhoea, are also vulnerable.

Recognition
As the condition develops, there may be:
◆ Headache, dizziness, and confusion.
◆ Loss of appetite, and nausea.
◆ Sweating, with pale, clammy skin.
◆ Cramps in the arms, legs, or the abdominal wall.
◆ Rapid, weakening pulse and breathing.

TREATMENT

YOUR AIMS ARE:
■ To replace lost fluid and salt.
■ To cool down the casualty if necessary.

1 Help the casualty to a cool place. Lay him down and raise his legs.

2 Give water; follow, if possible, with weak salt solution (one teaspoon of salt per litre of water).

3 Even if he recovers quickly, ensure he sees a doctor.

IF responses deteriorate, place him in the recovery position (*see page 12*).

☎ *DIAL 999 FOR AN AMBULANCE.*

Record breathing, pulse, and response every ten minutes; be ready to resuscitate if needed (*see pages 8–22*).

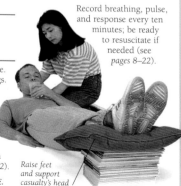

Raise feet and support casualty's head

HEATSTROKE

This is caused by a failure of the brain's "thermostat". The body can be overheated by fever or prolonged exposure to heat. It can follow heat exhaustion when sweating stops and the body is not cooled by evaporation. It can occur suddenly, causing loss of consciousness in minutes. This may be signalled by feeling uneasy and ill.

Recognition
- Headache, dizziness, and discomfort.
- Restlessness and confusion.
- Hot, flushed, and dry skin.
- A rapid deterioration in the level of response (*see page 128*).
- A full, bounding pulse.
- Body temperature above 40°C (104°F).

TREATMENT

YOUR AIMS ARE:
- To lower the casualty's body temperature as quickly as possible.
- To arrange removal of the casualty to hospital.

1 Quickly move casualty to a cool place. Remove outer clothing if possible.
☎ **DIAL 999 FOR AN AMBULANCE.**

TAKING A TEMPERATURE
- Hold thermometer at opposite end from the silver mercury bulb.
- Shake the thermometer, ensuring that the mercury drops well below the normal mark, 37°C (98.6°F).
- Place under tongue (or armpit for a child) for three minutes. Read temperature where mercury stops.

IF the casualty's responses deteriorate, or he becomes unconscious, open the airway and check breathing; be prepared to resuscitate if necessary (*see pages 8–22*). Place him in the recovery position (*see page 12*).

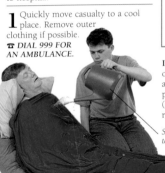

Sprinkle sheet with water to keep it cool

Wrap casualty in wet sheet

2 Wrap him in a cold, wet sheet until his temperature falls to 38°C / 100.4°F (tongue) or 37.5°C / 99.5°F (armpit). If no sheet is available, fan the casualty or sponge him with cold water.

3 When the temperature falls to a safe level, replace wet sheet with a dry one. Monitor casualty until help arrives. If the temperature rises again, repeat cooling process (*see step 2*).

FOREIGN BODIES

9

A ny object, large or small, that enters the body either through a wound or body orifice, such as the ear, nose, eye, vagina, or rectum, is a "foreign body". These are often specks of dirt or grit and can rest on, or enter, the eye. These injuries are not usually serious, but can be distressing and painful for the casualty. Reassuring, calm, and prompt treatment is essential.

Understanding treatment procedures

This chapter explains how to treat foreign bodies in the skin, eye, nose, and ear, and gives advice on what to do when an object is swallowed or inhaled.

Casualties with foreign bodies in ano-genital orifices should receive medical help. For advice on foreign bodies embedded in wounds, see page 50.

FIRST-AID PRIORITIES

♦ Decide whether it is possible to remove the foreign body. If the object cannot be removed safely, or if you are unsure, obtain medical help.

♦ If the foreign body can be removed, reassure the casualty and ask him or her to keep still. It may be necessary to be quite firm.

♦ Once the object has been removed, take any necessary further action. If you suspect a risk of infection or internal injury, seek a doctor's advice.

Foreign Bodies in the Skin

Small foreign bodies, such as wood splinters, cause little or no bleeding. If part of an object protrudes, try to draw it out. If it is deeply embedded, do not remove it as you may cause further injury. An object in a wound may attract bacteria and dirt. Clean the wound; check that tetanus immunisation is up to date.

See also:
Foreign Bodies in Minor Wounds, *page 50*.
Severe External Bleeding, *page 40*.

Splinters

Small splinters of wood, metal, or glass in the skin, particularly of the hands, feet, and knees, are common injuries. The splinter can usually be drawn out using tweezers. If it is deeply embedded, lies over a joint, or is difficult to remove, leave it and tell the casualty to consult a doctor.

TREATMENT

YOUR AIMS ARE:
- To remove the splinter.
- To minimise the risk of infection.

> **DO NOT** probe the wound with a sharp object, such as a needle, in an attempt to lever out the splinter.

1 Gently clean the area around the splinter with soap and warm water. Sterilise a pair of tweezers by passing them through a flame.

IF the splinter does not come out easily, or breaks, treat it as an embedded foreign body (*see page 50*), and seek medical advice.

Pull out splinter in straight line, along track of entry

2 Grasp the splinter with the tweezers as close to the skin as possible, and draw it out at the angle it went in.

Encourage bleeding to flush out remaining dirt

3 Squeeze the wound to encourage a little bleeding. Clean the area and apply an adhesive dressing (plaster).

4 Check that tetanus immunisation is up to date. If not, or if in doubt, advise the casualty to see a doctor.

FISH HOOKS

Embedded fish hooks are difficult to draw out because of their barbs; you should only attempt to remove one if medical aid is not available. If you do remove it, advise the casualty to see a doctor if tetanus immunity is in doubt.

TREATMENT

YOUR AIMS ARE:
- To seek medical aid. If unavailable, to remove the fish hook without causing the casualty any further injury and pain.

WHEN MEDICAL AID IS EXPECTED

1 Cut the fishing line as close as possible to the hook.

Ensure top of padding is level with top of hook

2 Build up pads of gauze around the hook until you can bandage over it without pushing it in further.

Do not bandage too tightly

3 Bandage over padding and hook; try not to press on the hook. Ensure casualty gets medical care.

WHEN MEDICAL AID IS NOT READILY AVAILABLE

If the barb is visible

> **DO NOT** pull out a hook unless the barb is cut off.

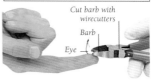

Cut barb with wirecutters

Barb

Eye

1 Cut the barb away then carefully withdraw the hook by its eye.

2 Clean the wound, then pad around it with gauze and bandage it. Ensure tetanus immunity is up to date.

If the barb is not visible

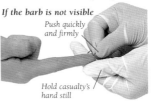

Push quickly and firmly

Hold casualty's hand still

1 If possible, push the hook forwards through the wound, until the barb emerges from the skin.

2 Cut away barb, then withdraw the hook, and dress wound as above.

FOREIGN BODIES IN THE EYE

A speck of dust, loose eyelash, or a contact lens can literally float on the white of the eye, and is usually easily removed. However, anything that sticks to the eye, penetrates the eyeball, or rests on the coloured part of the eye (the *pupil* and *iris*) should not be touched.

Recognition *There may be:*
◆ Blurred vision.
◆ Pain or discomfort.
◆ Redness and watering of the eye.
◆ Eyelids screwed up in spasm.

See also:
Eye Wounds, *page 44.*

TREATMENT

YOUR AIM IS:
■ To prevent injury to the eye.

1 Advise the casualty not to rub her eye. Sit her down facing the light.

> **DO NOT** touch anything sticking to, or embedded in, the eyeball, or the coloured part of the eye.

2 Gently separate the eyelids with your finger and thumb. Examine every part of her eye.

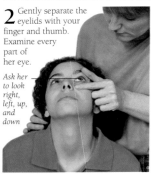

Ask her to look right, left, up, and down

IF the foreign body is sticking to or embedded in the eye, cover the eye with an eye pad and a bandage, then take or send the casualty to hospital.

3 If you see an object on the white of the eye, pour clean water from a glass or eyebath into corner of the eye.

4 If this is unsuccessful, providing the foreign body is not stuck in place, lift it off with a moist swab, or the damp corner of a tissue or clean handkerchief.

Ask casualty to pull down upper lid; lower lashes may brush particle clear

IF the object is under the upper eyelid, ask her to grasp her lashes and pull the lid over the lower lid. Blinking under water may make the object float clear.

FOREIGN BODIES IN THE NOSE

Young children may push small objects up their noses. These can cause blockage and infection and, if sharp, may damage the tissues of the nostrils. Do not try to extricate these items; you may cause injury or push the object in further.

Recognition *There may be:*
◆ Difficulty in breathing, or noisy breathing through the nose.
◆ Swelling of the nose.
◆ Smelly or blood-stained discharge; this may indicate an object that has been lodged for some time.

TREATMENT

YOUR AIM IS:
■ To obtain medical attention.

1 Keep the casualty quiet and calm. Tell him or her to breathe through the mouth at a normal rate.

> **DO NOT** attempt to remove the foreign body with your fingers or any instrument, even if you can see it.

2 Arrange to take or send the casualty to hospital.

FOREIGN BODIES IN THE EAR

An object lodged in the ear can block the ear canal and cause temporary deafness, or may damage the ear-drum. Young children often push objects into their ears; people leave cotton wool in the ear after cleaning it. Insects can fly or crawl into the ear and may cause alarm.

TREATMENT

YOUR AIMS ARE:
■ To prevent injury to the ear.
■ To obtain medical attention for a lodged foreign body.
■ To remove a trapped insect.

FOR A LODGED FOREIGN BODY

> **DO NOT** attempt to remove the object. You may cause serious injury and push it in even further.

Arrange to take or send the casualty to hospital as soon as possible. Reassure the casualty during the journey, or until medical help arrives.

FOR AN INSECT IN THE EAR

1 Reassure the casualty, and sit her down.

Support head with affected ear uppermost

2 Gently flood the ear with tepid water so that the insect floats out.

3 If this is unsuccessful, take or send the casualty to hospital.

SWALLOWED FOREIGN BODIES

Small objects such as coins, safety pins, or buttons can easily be swallowed by young children. If the object is sharp, it may damage the digestive tract. Small, smooth objects are unlikely to cause this type of injury, but they are still dangerous as they can lead to choking.
See also:
Choking Baby and Child, *page 26.*

TREATMENT

YOUR AIM IS:
■ To obtain medical attention.

FOR SHARP OR LARGE OBJECTS
☎ *DIAL 999 FOR AN AMBULANCE.*
Reassure the casualty while waiting for medical help to arrive.

> **DO NOT** give the casualty anything to eat or drink – an anaesthetic may be administered at hospital.

FOR SMALL, SMOOTH OBJECTS
Reassure the casualty, and take or send him to hospital or to a doctor.

INHALED FOREIGN BODIES

Small, smooth objects can slip past the throat's protective mechanisms into air passages. Dry peanuts pose a particular danger to young children as they can be inhaled into the lungs, causing serious damage. Some people are allergic to nuts, which can cause anaphylactic shock (*see page 35*).

Recognition
◆ Some sign or noise of choking, which quickly passes.
◆ A persistent dry cough.
◆ Difficulty in breathing.
See also:
Choking,
pages 24–7.

TREATMENT

YOUR AIM IS:
■ To obtain urgent medical attention.

1 Treat the casualty for choking, if necessary (*see pages 24–7*).
☎ *DIAL 999 FOR AN AMBULANCE.*

2 Reassure the casualty while waiting for the ambulance. Try to discover from him or any bystanders what kind of foreign body has been inhaled, and inform the medical services.

Choking child
If back slaps and chest thrusts fail, apply abdominal thrusts.

Hold child around central upper abdomen and give up to five quick, upward thrusts

POISONING, BITES, AND STINGS

10

Poisoning can be accidental or deliberate (attempted suicide); it is caused by food, drugs, or alcohol. Common sense can prevent many bites and stings; animals and insects may attack if injured or provoked.

Recognising and treating poisoning
Effects depend on the type and amount of poison. Poisoning is usually treatable. Try to identify the poison; look for clues, such as tablets. This chapter deals with the types of poisoning most often encountered by a First Aider, such as acute poisoning.

When bites and stings need medical help
Stings are often minor, and first aid alone relieves pain. Bites, however, need medical attention. After dressing a bite, ensure that the casualty's tetanus injection is up to date. Be aware that, even in death, the venom of some animals is still active.

FIRST-AID PRIORITIES
◆ Be ready to resuscitate if necessary.

◆ Prevent further injury: SWALLOWED POISONS: do not induce vomiting. INHALED POISONS: do not endanger yourself; remove casualty from danger. ABSORBED POISONS: wash chemicals off skin. BITES AND STINGS: move casualty to safety; tend cuts.

◆ Obtain appropriate medical help.

HOUSEHOLD POISONS

Most households contain potentially poisonous substances, such as paint stripper, bleach, dishwasher detergent, and weedkiller. These can be spilled, causing chemical burns, or swallowed, causing poisoning. Children in particular are at risk from poisoning by household products.

See also:
Chemical Burns, *page 90.*
Drug Poisoning, *page 108.*

HOW TO PREVENT POISONING
◆ Keep toxic chemicals out of children's reach and sight. ◆ Lock up medicines. ◆ Leave poisonous substances in original containers. Do not store poisons in soft-drinks bottles; children may drink them.
◆ Buy medicines and household substances in child-resistant containers. ◆ Dispose of unwanted medicines appropriately.

TREATMENT

YOUR AIMS ARE:
■ To maintain the airway, breathing, and circulation.
■ To remove any contaminated clothing.
■ To identify the poison.
■ To obtain medical aid.

FOR SWALLOWED POISONS

1 Check and, if necessary, clear the casualty's airway (*see page 11*).

To use a face shield, place the oval tube between the casualty's teeth. Seal your lips around the top of the tube to begin mouth-to-mouth respiration.

Pinch shield over nose

Blow until chest rises

IF the casualty becomes unconscious, check breathing and be prepared to resuscitate (*see pages 8–22*). Place him in the recovery position (*see page 12*).

IF you need to give mouth-to-mouth ventilation and there are chemicals on the casualty's mouth, use a plastic face shield, if possible, to protect yourself.

NEVER attempt to induce vomiting.

---

2 ☎ *DIAL 999 FOR AN AMBULANCE* or call a doctor. Give information about the swallowed poison, if possible.

IF a conscious casualty's lips are burned by corrosive substances, give him frequent sips of cold water or milk.

ALCOHOL POISONING

Alcohol depresses the central nervous system. Prolonged intake impairs physical and mental abilities, and unconsciousness may ensue.

Dangers of alcohol poisoning

◆ An unconscious casualty risks inhaling and choking on vomit.
◆ Alcohol dilates the blood vessels, so hypothermia may develop if the casualty is exposed to cold.
◆ A casualty with head injuries who smells of alcohol may not receive the appropriate treatment.

Recognition

◆ A strong smell of alcohol.
◆ Unconsciousness: casualty may be roused, but will quickly relapse.
◆ A flushed, moist face. ◆ Deep, noisy breathing. ◆ A bounding pulse.
In the later stages of unconsciousness:
◆ A dry, bloated appearance to the face. ◆ Shallow breathing. ◆ Dilated pupils that react poorly to light.
◆ A weak, rapid pulse.

See also:
Hypothermia, *page 95.*

TREATMENT

YOUR AIMS ARE:
■ To maintain an open airway.
■ To seek medical attention for the casualty if it is appropriate.

IF the casualty is unconscious, open airway and check breathing; be ready to resuscitate (*see pages 8–22*). Place in recovery position (*see page 12*).

IF in doubt or you suspect head injury, ☎ DIAL 999 FOR AN AMBULANCE.

2 Protect the casualty from cold, if possible; insulate him from the ground and cover him.

Shake and shout:
"Can you hear me?"
or "Open your
eyes!"

1 Check level of consciousness. Gently shake the casualty's shoulders and speak to him loudly and clearly to see if he responds.

Watch him in case
he becomes
unconscious

Put a
coat or
blanket
over
him

DRUG POISONING

This results from an accidental or deliberate overdose of prescribed or over-the-counter drugs, or from drug abuse. The signs of poisoning vary depending on the type of drug and how it is taken (*see chart below*).

TREATMENT

YOUR AIMS ARE:
- To maintain the airway, breathing, and circulation.
- To arrange removal to hospital.

1 Check and, if necessary, clear the casualty's airway (*see page 11*).

IF unconscious, check breathing and pulse, and be ready to resuscitate if necessary (*see pages 8–22*).

2 Place the casualty in the recovery position (*see page 12*).

> **DO NOT** induce vomiting. It can be ineffective and cause more harm.

3 ☎ *DIAL 999 FOR AN AMBULANCE.* Keep samples of vomit. Look for clues to the drug's identity, such as containers or "suicide" notes. Send these with the casualty to hospital.

DRUG	EFFECTS
Painkillers: Aspirin	• Upper abdominal pain, nausea, and vomiting (possibly blood-stained) • Ringing in the ears • "Sighing" when breathing • Confusion and delirium
Painkillers: Paracetamol	• Little effect at first • Later, features of liver damage: upper abdominal pain and tenderness, nausea, and vomiting
Nervous system depressants and tranquillisers: such as barbiturates and valium	• Lethargy and sleepiness, leading to unconsciousness • Shallow breathing • A weak, irregular, or abnormally slow or fast pulse
Stimulants and hallucinogens Amphetamines (such as Ecstasy) and LSD (commonly swallowed); cocaine (commonly inhaled or "snorted")	• Excitable, hyperactive behaviour, wildness, and frenzy • Sweating • Tremor of the hands • Hallucinations: the casualty may be "hearing" voices or "seeing" things
Narcotics (commonly injected) Morphine, heroin	• Constricted pupils • Sluggishness and confusion, possibly leading to unconsciousness • Slow, shallow breathing, which may cease • Needle marks may be infected, or infection introduced by dirty needles
Solvents (commonly inhaled) Glue, lighter fuel	• Nausea, vomiting, and headaches • Hallucinations • Possibly, unconsciousness • Rarely, cardiac arrest

FOOD POISONING

This may be caused by eating food containing bacteria or by toxins produced by bacteria already in food.

Types of food poisoning

Bacterial food poisoning is often caused by the *Salmonella* group of bacteria (associated with farm animals). Symptoms may appear rapidly or be delayed for a day or so.

Toxic food poisoning is frequently caused by toxins produced by the bacteria group of Staphylococcus. Symptoms usually develop rapidly, possibly within two to six hours.

See also:
Shock, page 32.

Recognition

- Nausea and vomiting.
- Cramping abdominal pains.
- Diarrhoea (possibly bloodstained).
- Headache or fever.
- Features of shock.
- Collapse.

PREVENTING FOOD POISONING

- Ensure frozen poultry and meat are fully defrosted before cooking.
- Cook meat, poultry, fish, and eggs thoroughly to kill bacteria. ◆ Never keep food lukewarm for long.
- Wash hands before preparing food. ◆ Wear protective gloves or waterproof plasters if you have cuts.

TREATMENT

YOUR AIMS ARE:
- To encourage the casualty to rest.
- To seek medical advice or aid.
- To give the casualty plenty of bland fluids to drink.

1 Help the casualty to lie down and rest. Call a doctor for advice.

Give bland fluids like water or diluted fruit juice

Keep casualty warm

2 Give the casualty plenty to drink, and a bowl to use if she vomits.

IF the casualty's condition worsens, ☎ *DIAL 999 FOR AN AMBULANCE.*

ANIMAL BITES

Bites from sharp teeth cause puncture wounds that carry germs into the tissues. Human bites also crush the tissues. Hitting teeth with a fist can produce a "bite" wound at the knuckles. Any bite that breaks the skin causes a wound vulnerable to infection. A bite needs prompt first aid and medical attention.
See also:
Minor Wounds, *page 49.*
Severe External Bleeding, *page 40.*

TREATMENT

YOUR AIMS ARE:
■ To control bleeding.
■ To minimise the risk of infection, both to the casualty and yourself.
■ To obtain medical attention.

FOR SERIOUS WOUNDS

1 Control bleeding by applying direct pressure and raising the injured part.

2 Cover the wound with a sterile dressing or a clean pad bandaged in place.

Wear protective gloves if possible

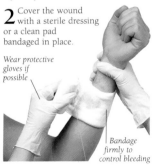

Bandage firmly to control bleeding

3 Arrange to take or send the casualty to hospital.

FOR SUPERFICIAL BITES

1 Wash the wound thoroughly with soap and warm water.

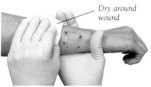

Dry around wound

2 Pat the wound dry with clean gauze swabs and cover with an adhesive dressing or a small sterile dressing.

3 Advise the casualty to see a doctor in case inoculation is needed.

POTENTIAL INFECTIONS

Rabies is a potentially fatal infection spread in the saliva of infected animals. If bitten abroad, or by a smuggled animal, the casualty must receive anti-rabies injections and the animal be examined. Seek police help to secure a suspect animal.

There is only a small risk of hepatitis B or C being transmitted via a human bite and even less risk with HIV. If concerned about the risk of infection, get medical advice.

INSECT STINGS

Bee, wasp, and hornet stings tend to be more painful than dangerous. An initial sharp pain is followed by mild swelling and soreness, which first aid can relieve. Some people are allergic to stings and can rapidly develop the serious condition of anaphylactic shock. Multiple stings can also be dangerous. Stings in the mouth or throat are serious, as swelling can obstruct the airway.

See also:
Anaphylactic Shock, *page 35.*
Breathing Difficulties, *page 29.*

TREATMENT

YOUR AIMS ARE:
■ To relieve swelling and pain.
■ To remove to hospital if necessary.

FOR A STING IN THE SKIN

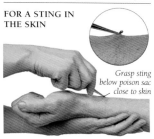

Grasp sting below poison sac close to skin

IF there are signs of anaphylactic shock,
☎ *DIAL 999 FOR AN AMBULANCE*

1 If the sting is still in the wound, pluck it out firmly with fine tweezers.

2 Apply a cold compress (*see page 119*) to relieve pain and swelling. Advise casualty to see his doctor if these persist.

FOR A STING IN THE MOUTH

1 Give the casualty ice to suck or cold water to sip, to minimise swelling.
☎ *DIAL 999 FOR AN AMBULANCE.*
Reassure the casualty.

TICK BITES

These tiny, spider-like creatures are found in grass or woodlands. They suck blood from animals and humans. An unfed tick is small and hard to see, especially as its bite is painless, but when sucking blood, it swells to the size of a pea and is easy to see. Ticks cause infection and disease, so remove one as soon as possible; put it in a container and ask the casualty to take it to a doctor for analysis.

Lever tick out carefully

Removing a tick
Using tweezers, grasp head close to the skin. Use a to-and-fro action to lever out head. Mouthparts will be embedded in the skin; avoid breaking the tick and leaving the head behind.

MARINE STINGS

Sea creatures cause different types of injury. Jellyfish have stinging cells that release poison. Other marine life have spines that puncture skin. Most marine life in temperate climates is not very poisonous.

TREATMENT FOR STINGS

YOUR AIMS ARE:
■ To reassure the casualty.
■ To inactivate stinging cells before they release their venom, and to neutralise any free venom.
■ To relieve pain and discomfort.

1 Reassure the casualty and sit him down. Pour copious amounts of vinegar or sea water over the injury to incapacitate stinging cells that have not yet released venom.

Pour vinegar on to wound

DO NOT rub alcohol or sand on to the affected area of skin as this may aggravate the injury.

2 Dust a dry powder over the skin around the affected area to make any remaining stinging cells stick together. Talcum powder is good for this. Meat tenderiser, used in barbecue cooking, is also good as it contains papain, which inactivates venom.

3 Gently brush off the powder with a clean, non-fluffy pad.

IF the injuries are severe, or there is a serious general reaction (*see page 35*), ☎ *DIAL 999 FOR AN AMBULANCE.*

IF the casualty is having difficulty breathing, she may be in anaphylactic shock; treat as described on page 35.

TREATMENT FOR PUNCTURE WOUNDS

YOUR AIMS ARE:
■ To inactivate the venom.
■ To obtain medical aid.

1 Put the injured part in hot water for at least 30 minutes. Top up water as it cools, being careful not to scald the casualty.

2 Take or send the casualty to hospital, where spines remaining in the skin may have to be removed.

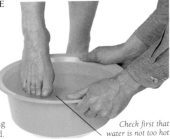

Check first that water is not too hot